PF for NetBSD, FreeBSD,
DragonFly, and OpenBSD

The OpenBSD PF
Packet Filter Book

Published by Reed Media Services

The OpenBSD PF Packet Filter Book:
PF for NetBSD, FreeBSD, DragonFly, and OpenBSD
August 2006

Publisher: Reed Media Services
Book Editor: Jeremy C. Reed

ISBN 978-0-9790342-0-6

Contents

Forward

Welcome to The OpenBSD PF Packet Filter Book which covers PF for NetBSD, FreeBSD, DragonFly, and, of course, OpenBSD. This book is based on the *PF: The OpenBSD Packet Filter* documentation by Nick Holland and Joel Knight and many other OpenBSD developers and users.

The original set of HTML documents is intended as a general introduction to the PF system as run specifically on the latest official release of OpenBSD. The original document is available at http://www.openbsd.org/faq/pf/. Different versions of PF are available for various BSD platforms. And as PF is always growing and developing, the reader is advised to read the man pages for the version of PF they are currently working with. This documentation is intended to be used as a supplement to the man pages, and not as a replacement for them. For a complete and in-depth view of what PF can do, please start by reading the technical pf(4) man page.

This documentation was edited, slightly reordered and rewritten, formatted for printing, cross-referenced, indexed, and prepared for easy-to-follow book reading by Jeremy C. Reed. Also content was rewritten and new content added to cover the other BSD operating systems. In addition, graphics were created to replace the original text-based diagrams. The content of this book – including changes and additions – is available under the original license. As appropriate, improvements were sent upstream to the original copyright owners for the OpenBSD documentation and shared for documentation for the FreeBSD, NetBSD, and DragonFly projects.

The longer configuration examples, rulesets, and scripts from this book are available for download via http://www.reedmedia.net/books/pf-book/.

Portions of the sales of this printed and bound book will be donated to the OpenBSD project. Also please consider donating to the

OpenBSD project; please visit
http://www.openbsd.org/donations.html.

Acknowledgements

Thank you to Bruno Afonso, Pavel Cahyna, Liam J. Foy, Bryan Irvine, Peter Postma, Atom Powers, Jeff Rizzo, and Joachim Schipper for providing valuable feedback and information for this book.

This book is open source – see the cover page ii for the license. Many people have helped – from small fixes to major writing – with the original OpenBSD www/faq/pf documentation. Thank you to the following for helping with the PF documentation: Tomasz Bak, Henning Brauer, Pedro Cavaca, Steve Ewing, Stavros Filargiropoulos, Peter Fraser, Peter Gilman, David Goodrich, Moritz Grimm, Daniel Hartmeier, Nick Holland, Zoran Ivanic, Antoine Jacoutot, Matt Jibson, Saad Kadhi, Joel Knight, David Krause, Egbert Krook, Chad Loder, michelfc, Ryan McBride, Jason McIntyre, Steven Mestdagh, Otto Moerbeek, Nikos Ntarmos, Marco Peerebom, Mike Pennington, Daniel Polak, Jens Ropers, Tom Ryan, Justin Sabino, Xavier Santolaria, Steven Schubiger, Andreas Semborg, Margarida Sequeira, Chad Stewart, Trevor Talbot, Tamas Tevesz, Ken Weterback, and Jared Yanovich.

And thank you to the OpenBSD project for developing and maintaining the PF suite and documentation.

1. Introduction

1.1. Background

OpenBSD's Packet Filter, known as PF, was started by Daniel Hart-meier in June 2001.[1] At that time, stateful filtering and NAT were implemented and the ruleset syntax was identical to IPF, minus some options that were not yet implemented (such as keep frags and return-icmp).

By the end of June, 2001, it was integrated into the OpenBSD source code tree. PF is maintained and developed by Hartmeier and the rest of the OpenBSD team.

1.2. Versions

PF itself does not have an official version, but the new official release corresponds with the OpenBSD release. To help keep track of different PF features, the versions used throughout this book will correspond with the OpenBSD release version.

PF 3.0 (December 1, 2001)

First official release, included with OpenBSD 3.0: "A new packet filter, PF, featuring NAT capabilities, with a mostly ipf-compatible syntax."

PF 3.1 (May 19, 2002)

Various enhancements, including performance improvements and filtering protocols such as "esp". Also adds authpf, an utility for dynamically adding and removing filter rules when users login.

---

[1] IP Filter (IPF) was removed from OpenBSD on May 29, 2001.

PF 3.2 (November 1, 2002)

This release introduced "antispoof" keyword for spoofing protection, much simplified rule file language, extended filtering capabilities, per-rule granularity for state table entries, and dynamic interface expansion so rulesets do not need to be reloaded on IP changes.

PF 3.3 (May 1, 2003)

Many improvements in PF 3.3, including merging of ALTQ with PF so the packet filter is used to assign packets to queues and the altq.conf configuration is gone.[2] Also includes parser improvements to allow more optional parts and to make rules shorter and more human readable. Other additions were: anchors to allow subrulesets which can be loaded and modified independently; tables support for large address lists in rules; load balancing by doing NAT or redirection to multiple addresses; TCP window scaling support; full CIDR support; early checksum verification return on invalid packets; and spamd, the spam deferral daemon.

PF 3.4 (Nov 1, 2003)

This version introduced adaptive state timeouts to prevent state table overflows attacks, SYN flood attack protection, filtering on tags (added by bridge based on MAC addresses), stateful TCP normalization to prevent NAT detection and uptime calculation, and passive operating system detection.

PF 3.5 (May 1, 2004)

PF 3.5 is included with FreeBSD 5.x and DragonFly 1.2, 1.4, and 1.6.

This version of PF had many changes, including: inverted the socket match order when redirecting to localhost (to prevent a potential security problem of remote connections being identified as local); added sticky-address load balancing, atomic commits of ruleset

---

[2]Some other BSDs may not have ALTQ integrated with PF yet or may use the original ALTQ framework. Read the appropriate sections for your BSD flavour and also section 12.3 for more details.

changes; a 30% reduction in state table entries size; and limiting number of clients and states per client using source-tracking. Also, CARP (the Common Address Redundancy Protocol) was added for filtering gateway failover by allowing multiple machines to share responsibility for IP addresses. And additions to the pfsync(4) interface allow it to synchronize state table entries between multiple firewalls. Also, pflogd(8) gained privilege separation and authpf(8) could tag traffic in pflog(4) so users can be associated with traffic through a NAT setup.

PF 3.6 (November 1, 2004)

PF 3.6 is included with NetBSD 3.0.

Changes include: PF can add received prefixes to a pf(4) table (for BGP), pfctl(8) provides a rules optimizer to help improve filtering speed, and nested anchors.

PF 3.7 (May 19, 2005)

This version is included with FreeBSD 6.0 and NetBSD 4.0.

This release included: improved error messages and more statistics counters, automatically adding flooding IP addresses to tables and flushing states, tagging of all packets matching state entries, "skip" keyword for skipping arbitrary interfaces (like loopback), limiting TCP connections by establishment rate, and filtering on route(8) labels[3].

PF 3.8 (November 1, 2005)

The main change in PF 3.8 is that it can filter based on routing information from OpenBSD's bgpd. Also, more logging details were added.

PF 3.9 (May 1, 2006)

This version optimized performance, added dynamic interface group expansion, and the state, byte, and packet counters were raised to 64

---

[3]Filtering on route(8) labels is not working on all operating systems; for example, DragonFly and NetBSD do not have labels for routes.

bit. And pfsync can attach states to their rules.

Also OpenBSD added tftp-proxy, a PF proxy for the TFTP protocol.

2. Getting Started

2.1. Activating PF

The pfctl command is used for controlling the packet filter. It can configure rulesets, list NAT sessions, retrieve PF status, and a lot more. Many of its options and features will be covered throughout this book.

You can activate and deactivate PF by using the pfctl(8) program:

```
# pfctl -e
# pfctl -d
```

to enable and disable, respectively. Note that this just enables or disables PF, it doesn't actually load a ruleset. The ruleset must be loaded separately, either before or after PF is enabled.

When PF is enabled, it has an open policy. Nevertheless, even when no block rules are loaded, PF will block packets with IP Options by default – see section 6.14 for details.

Depending on your system, you may need to load a pf kernel module first. Read the following section for your operating system if needed.

If you plan on routing packets, remember to enable IP forwarding between interfaces – see section 7.4 for details.

2.2. OpenBSD

To activate PF on OpenBSD and have it read its configuration file at boot, add the line

```
pf=YES
```

to the file /etc/rc.conf.local. Reboot your system to have it take effect.

OpenBSD has some temporary rules that are initially loaded before starting up the networking. These default rules first block all, allow loopback, allow SSH connections, allow DNS lookups (so it can later properly boot rulesets using DNS addresses), allow pings, and allow pfsync and carp. If using IPv6, it allows neighbor and router advertisement and solicitation. And if using NFS, it is allowed also. These rules are only active until the real PF configuration is loaded.

2.3. NetBSD

PF was integrated in NetBSD in July 2004 and the first supported release was NetBSD 3.0. NetBSD 3.0 includes PF 3.6 plus some patches from the OPENBSD_3_6 branch. NetBSD 4.0 includes PF from OpenBSD 3.7 with patches from the OPENBSD_3_7 branch. NetBSD 2.x does not have support for PF in the base system; nevertheless a LKM (Loadable Kernel Module) for PF is also available for NetBSD 2.x via the pkgsrc/security/pflkm package.[1] PF is not available for NetBSD 1.6 or older. CARP support is available in NetBSD 4.0.

NetBSD Kernel Configuration

To use PF, you do not need to compile your own kernel. You can use the /usr/lkm/pf.o kernel module. Use modload(8) to load the LKM:

```
# modload /usr/lkm/pf.o
```

To load the LKM at boot time, you need to set lkm=YES in /etc/rc.conf and add the following line to /etc/lkm.conf:

```
/usr/lkm/pf.o - - - - AFTERMOUNT
```

But if you prefer to use PF in the kernel, the following pseudo-devices should be added to the kernel configuration:

---

[1] See the *PF loadable kernel module for NetBSD 2* webpage at http://nedbsd.nl/~ppostma/pf/ for more information.

```
pseudo-device pf      # PF packet filter
pseudo-device pflog   # PF log interface
```

If you're not interested in logging packets with PF, then you could leave out the pflog device. Also you need at least the following option enabled:

```
options PFIL_HOOKS # pfil(9) packet filter hooks
```

This packet filter interface allows any packet filter to work without kernel modifications.[2] This PFIL_HOOKS option should be enabled in NetBSD's GENERIC kernel by default.

To enable packet filtering on a bridge, the following line should be added to the NetBSD kernel configuration:[3]

```
options BRIDGE_IPF # bridge uses IP/IPv6 pfil hooks
```

To also build with CARP include:

```
device carp      # Common Address Redundancy Protocol
```

You need to recompile, install and boot the new kernel for the settings to take effect.

Enabling PF on NetBSD

To enable PF at boot time on NetBSD, set pf=YES in /etc/rc.conf. It is important to note that the boot procedure will be aborted, if the PF configuration file doesn't exist. The default configuration file is /etc/pf.conf. This can be changed by setting the pf_rules variable in /etc/rc.conf.

To start, stop, restart, reload or list filter information, you can use the /etc/rc.d/pf script.

To enable pflogd(8) at boot time, set pflogd=YES in /etc/rc.conf. To start, stop or restart pflogd(8) manually, you can use the /etc/rc.d/pflogd rc.d script.

---

[2]This pfil(9) framework was added over seven years before a second packet filter was included with NetBSD.

[3]See page 110 for more details on using bridging on NetBSD.

NetBSD also provides an initial temporary configuration file used during the network configuration to protect the machine from possible attacks. (This is when PF is enabled in the rc.conf file.) Later during the boot, your real rules are loaded. These temporary rules provide a default deny, allow loopback, allow outgoing DNS (needed later by pfctl to resolve names), allow outgoing ping requests (which might be needed by dhclient to validate leases), and allow IPv6 router/neighbor solicitation and advertisement. This default configuration is at /etc/defaults/pf.boot.conf (and is loaded by /etc/rc.d/pf_boot). You can override the default initial configuration by creating a file named /etc/pf.boot.conf.[4] Please read the pf.boot.conf(5) manual page for more information. Note: This is specific to NetBSD.

Differences with OpenBSD

The usage of PF in NetBSD is basically the same as in OpenBSD, but there are a few differences. Most of them are missing features.

- ALTQ is not supported by PF by default. Enabling it in the kernel will result in compilation errors. You can only use ALTQ by using PF as LKM and having ALTQ enabled in the kernel. There's ongoing work in NetBSD to make a decent ALTQ API and change PF to use that API.[5]

- pfsync(4) is not supported (due to protocol number assignment issues). This will hopefully be solved in a future release.

- The carp(4) pseudo-device is not available in the default kernel. It can be enabled as shown in the NetBSD kernel configuration above. Or an alternative userland implementation, ucarp, can be installed via pkgsrc for CARP.

- The `group` keyword does nothing, because NetBSD doesn't keep the GID in its socket structure. This issue will probably be solved in a future release.

---

[4]Do not edit the /etc/defaults/ files, because they may be replaced during system upgrades.

[5]See the *ALTQ patches for NetBSD* webpage at http://nedbsd.nl/~ppostma/pf/altq.html.

- Filtering on route labels is not working, NetBSD doesn't have labels for routes. It is unknown whether this will be supported in a future release or not.

- spamd is not provided with the default installation of NetBSD. It is available via pkgsrc (mail/spamd).[6]

2.4. FreeBSD

PF was first officially released as part of FreeBSD 5.3 in November 2004. FreeBSD 6.1 includes PF 3.7 and FreeBSD 5.5 includes PF 3.5. FreeBSD 4.x does not include PF, but it is available via the security/pf port.

FreeBSD Kernel Configuration

By default on FreeBSD, PF is available as a kernel loadable module, which can be easily loaded with:

```
# kldload pf
```

The kernel module is enabled with pflog(4) logging, but without pf-sync and without ALTQ support. The /etc/rc.d/pf script will load the kernel module as needed at boot time.

To build a FreeBSD kernel with PF builtin, use the following kernel configurations:

```
device   pf        # PF OpenBSD packet-filter firewall
device   pflog     # logging support interface for PF
```

To also build with CARP and pfsync support, include:

```
device   carp      # Common Address Redundancy Protocol
device   pfsync    # synchronization interface for PF
```

You need to recompile, install and boot the new kernel for the settings to take effect.

---

[6]See chapter 19 for more information about spamd.

Enabling PF on FreeBSD

To start PF at boot time, set the variable

```
pf_enable=YES
```

in your /etc/rc.conf file. You can also define `pf_rules` to point to your custom rule file; it defaults to /etc/pf.conf which provides a commented-out example.

The /etc/rc.d/pf script includes command line arguments to start, stop, restart, reload, resync, and to show PF status.

To enable the PF logging, set `pflog_enable=YES` in your /etc/rc.conf file. The /etc/rc.d/pflog rc.d script can be used to start and stop the packet filter logging daemon.

Differences with OpenBSD

- The pfsync device for monitoring state changes is not part of FreeBSD's default loadable module. A custom kernel must be built with the pfsync device.

- ALTQ support is also not available with the default pf kernel module. A custom kernel can be built with ALTQ support. See page 83 for details.

- spamd is not provided with the default installation of FreeBSD. It is available via the FreeBSD ports (mail/spamd).

- The carp(4) pseudo-device is not available in the default kernel. It can be enabled as shown in the FreeBSD kernel configuration above. Also net/ucarp in the FreeBSD Ports provides a userland implementation of CARP.

2.5. DragonFly

PF was first officially released as part of DragonFly 1.2 in April 2005. DragonFly 1.4 and 1.6 include PF 3.5. It is mostly PF 3.6, but there are some minor differences.

DragonFly Kernel Configuration

By default on DragonFly, PF is available as a kernel loadable module, which can be loaded with:

```
# kldload pf
```

The kernel module is enabled with pflog(4) logging and without pf-sync and without ALTQ support. The /etc/rc.d/pf script will load the kernel module as needed at boot time.

To build a DragonFly kernel with a builtin PF, use the following kernel configurations:

```
device pf       # PF OpenBSD packet-filter firewall
device pflog    # logging support interface for PF
```

And to also build with pfsync support, include:

```
device pfsync  # synchronization interface for PF
```

You need to recompile, install and boot the new kernel for the settings to take effect.

Enabling PF on DragonFly

To start PF at boot time, set the variable

```
pf_enable=YES
```

in your /etc/rc.conf file. You can also define `pf_rules` to point to your custom rule file; it defaults to /etc/pf.conf which provides a commented-out empty example.

The /etc/rc.d/pf script includes command line arguments to start, stop, restart, reload, resync, and to show PF status.

To enable the PF logging, set `pflog_enable=YES` in your /etc/rc.conf file. The /etc/rc.d/pflog rc.d script can be used to start and stop the packet filter logging daemon.

11

Differences with OpenBSD

- No "set skip" option. (This is a PF 3.7 feature.)

- ALTQ is not available with the default DragonFly kernel. A custom kernel can be built with ALTQ support. See page 83 for details.

- The pfsync device for monitoring state changes is not part of DragonFly's default kernel module. A custom kernel can be built with pfsync device support. (See above.) DragonFly's ifconfig(8) does not support the pfsync device.

- The carp(4) device is not available. A userland implementation, ucarp, can be installed via pkgsrc for CARP.

- DragonFly does not have support for labels for routes. So filtering on route labels does not work. (This is a PF 3.7 feature.)

- spamd is not provided with the default installation of Dragon-Fly. It is available via the pkgsrc collection (mail/spamd).[7]

2.6. Controlling PF

After boot, PF operation can be managed using the pfctl(8) program. Some example commands follow:

Load the pf.conf file

```
# pfctl -f /etc/pf.conf
```

Parse the file, but don't load it

```
# pfctl -nf /etc/pf.conf
```

Load only the NAT rules from the file

```
# pfctl -Nf /etc/pf.conf
```

---

[7]See chapter 19 for more information about spamd.

Load only the filter rules from the file

```
# pfctl -Rf /etc/pf.conf
```

Show the current NAT rules

```
# pfctl -sn
```

Show the current filter rules

```
# pfctl -sr
```

Show the current state table

```
# pfctl -ss
```

Show filter stats and counters

```
# pfctl -si
```

Show everything it can show

```
# pfctl -sa
```

For a complete list of commands, please see the pfctl(8) man page.

3. Configuration Basics

3.1. pf.conf Configuration File

PF reads its configuration rules from /etc/pf.conf at boot time, as loaded by the rc scripts. Note that while /etc/pf.conf is the default filename and is loaded by the system rc scripts, it is just a text file[1] loaded and interpreted by pfctl(8) and inserted into pf(4). For some applications, other rulesets may be loaded from other files after boot. As with any well-designed Unix application, PF offers great flexibility.

The pf.conf file has seven optional and ordered parts:

- **Macros:** User-defined variables that can hold IP addresses, interface names, etc. This is introduced in chapter 4.

- **Tables:** A structure used to hold lists of IP addresses. This is covered in chapter 5.

- **Options:** Various options to control how PF works. This is covered in chapter 9 and in other sections.

- **Scrub:** Reprocessing packets to normalize and defragment them. See chapter 10 for details.

- **Queueing:** Provides bandwidth control and packet prioritization. This is covered in chapter 12.

- **Translation:** Controls Network Address Translation (NAT) and packet redirection. This is covered in chapters 7 and 8.

---

[1] There are pf.conf syntax and highlighting configurations available for some editors, such as vim and jed.

- **Filter Rules:** Allows the selective filtering or blocking of packets as they pass through any of the interfaces. And this is covered in chapter 6.

With the exception of macros and tables, each section should appear in this order in the configuration file, though not all sections have to exist for any particular application.

Blank lines are ignored, and lines beginning with a pound sign (#) are treated as comments. Long lines can be split up with a backslash character (\) to indicate that a continuation line follows. These conventions can help with the readability of the rules.

3.2. Addresses

Addresses can be specified as:

- A single IPv4 or IPv6 address.

- A CIDR network block.

- A fully qualified domain name that will be resolved via DNS when the ruleset is loaded. All resulting IP addresses will be substituted into the rule.

- The name of a network interface. Any IP addresses assigned to the interface will be substituted into the rule.

- The name of a network interface followed by */netmask* (i.e., /24). Each IP address on the interface is combined with the netmask to form a CIDR network block which is substituted into the rule.

- The name of a network interface in parentheses ( ). This tells PF to update the rule if the IP address(es) on the named interface change. This is useful on an interface that gets its IP address dynamically via DHCP or dial-up as the ruleset doesn't have to be reloaded each time the address changes.

- The name of a network interface followed by any one of these modifiers:

16

- ○ `:network` - substitutes the CIDR network block (e.g., 192.168.0.0/24)

- ○ `:broadcast` - substitutes the network broadcast address (e.g., 192.168.0.255)

- ○ `:peer` - substitutes the peer's IP address on a point-to-point link

  In addition, the :0 modifier can be appended to either an interface name or to any of the above modifiers to indicate that PF should not include aliased IP addresses in the substitution. These modifiers can also be used when the interface is contained in parentheses. Example: `fxp0:network:0`

- A table. (This is covered in chapter 5.)

- Any of the above but negated using the ! ("not") modifier.

- A set of addresses using a list. (This is covered in section 4.2.)

- The keyword `any` meaning all addresses.

- The keyword `all` which is short for `from any to any`.

3.3. Ports

Ports can be specified as:

- A number between 1 and 65535.

- A valid service name from /etc/services.

- A set of ports using a list. (This is covered in section 4.2.)

- A range:

`!=`	not equal
`<`	less than
`>`	greater than

<=	less than or equal
>=	greater than or equal
><	range
<>	inverse range

The last two are binary operators (they take two arguments) and do not include the arguments in the range.

:	inclusive range

The inclusive range operator is also a binary operator and does include the arguments in the range. (See the inclusive range examples on page 58.)

3.4. Protocols

The Layer 4 protocol of a packet can be specified as:

- `tcp`

- `udp`

- `icmp`

- `icmp6`

- A valid protocol name from /etc/protocols.

- A protocol number between 0 and 255 .

- A set of protocols using a list.

4. Lists and Macros

4.1. Overview

PF offers many ways in which a ruleset can be simplified. Some good examples are by using lists and macros for consolidating similar items and defining information. In addition, the ruleset language, or grammar, also offers some shortcuts for making a ruleset simpler. As a general rule of thumb, the simpler a ruleset is, the easier it is to understand and to maintain. Later chapters will introduce the actual ruleset syntax and actions.

4.2. Lists

A list allows the specification of multiple similar criteria within a rule. For example, multiple protocols, port numbers, addresses, etc. So, instead of writing one filter rule for each IP address that needs to be blocked, one rule can be written by specifying the IP addresses in a list. Lists are defined by specifying items within braces { }.

When pfctl(8) encounters a list during loading of the ruleset, it creates multiple rules, one for each item in the list. For example:

```
block out on fxp0 from { 192.168.0.1, \
  10.5.32.6 } to any
```

gets expanded to:

```
block out on fxp0 from 192.168.0.1 to any
block out on fxp0 from 10.5.32.6 to any
```

Multiple lists can be specified within a rule and are not limited to just filter rules:

```
rdr on fxp0 proto tcp from any to any \
  port { 22 80 } -> 192.168.0.6
block out on fxp0 proto { tcp udp } \
    from { 192.168.0.1, 10.5.32.6 } to any \
    port { ssh telnet }
```

Note that the commas between list items are optional.

Beware of constructs like the following, dubbed "negated lists", which are a common mistake:

```
pass in on fxp0 from { 10.0.0.0/8, !10.1.2.3 }
```

While the intended meaning is usually to match "any address within 10.0.0.0/8, except for 10.1.2.3", the rule expands to:

```
pass in on fxp0 from 10.0.0.0/8
pass in on fxp0 from !10.1.2.3
```

which matches any possible address. Instead, a table should be used (which is covered in upcoming chapter 5).

4.3. Macros

Macros are user-defined variables that can hold IP addresses, port numbers, interface names, etc. Macros can reduce the complexity of a PF ruleset and also make maintaining a ruleset much easier.

Macro names must start with a letter and may contain letters, digits, and underscores. Macro names cannot be reserved words such as pass, out, or queue.

```
ext_if = "fxp0"
block in on $ext_if from any to any
```

This creates a macro named ext_if. When a macro is referred to after it's been created, its name is preceded with a $ character.

Macros can also expand to lists, such as:

```
friends = "{ 192.168.1.1, 10.0.2.5, 192.168.43.53 }"
```

Macros can be defined recursively. Since macros are not expanded within quotes the following syntax must be used:

```
host1 = "192.168.1.1"
host2 = "192.168.1.2"
all_hosts = "{" $host1 $host2 "}"
```

The macro $all_hosts now expands to 192.168.1.1, 192.168.1.2.

4.4. Using Macros

Macros are useful because they provide an alternative to hard-coding addresses, port numbers, interfaces names, etc., into a ruleset. Did a server's IP address change? No problem, just update the macro; no need to mess around with the filter rules that you've spent time and energy perfecting for your needs.

A common convention in PF rulesets is to define a macro for each network interface. If a network card ever needs to be replaced with one that uses a different driver, for example swapping out a 3Com for an Intel, the macro can be updated and the filter rules will function as before. Another benefit is when installing the same ruleset on multiple machines. Certain machines may have different network cards in them, and using macros to define the network interfaces allows the rulesets to be installed with minimal editing. Using macros to define information in a ruleset that is subject to change, such as port numbers, IP addresses, and interface names, is recommended practice.

```
# define macros for each network interface
IntIF = "dc0"
ExtIF = "fxp0"
DmzIF = "fxp1"
```

Another common convention is using macros to define IP addresses and network blocks. This can greatly reduce the maintenance of a ruleset when IP addresses change.

```
# define our networks
IntNet = "192.168.0.0/24"
ExtAdd = "24.65.13.4"
DmzNet = "10.0.0.0/24"
```

If the internal network ever expanded or was renumbered into a different IP block, the macro can be updated:

```
IntNet = "{ 192.168.0.0/24, 192.168.1.0/24 }"
```

Once the ruleset is reloaded, everything will work as before.

4.5. More Examples

Let's look at a good set of rules to have in your ruleset to handle RFC 1918 addresses that just shouldn't be floating around the Internet, and when they are, are usually trying to cause trouble:

```
block in  quick on tl0 inet from 127.0.0.0/8 to any
block in  quick on tl0 inet from 192.168.0.0/16 to any
block in  quick on tl0 inet from 172.16.0.0/12 to any
block in  quick on tl0 inet from 10.0.0.0/8 to any
block out quick on tl0 inet from any to 127.0.0.0/8
block out quick on tl0 inet from any to 192.168.0.0/16
block out quick on tl0 inet from any to 172.16.0.0/12
block out quick on tl0 inet from any to 10.0.0.0/8
```

Now look at the following simplification:

```
block in  quick on tl0 inet from { 127.0.0.0/8, \
    192.168.0.0/16, 172.16.0.0/12, 10.0.0.0/8 } to any
block out quick on tl0 inet from any to { 127.0.0.0/8, \
    192.168.0.0/16, 172.16.0.0/12, 10.0.0.0/8 }
```

The ruleset has been reduced from eight lines down to two. Things get even better when macros are used in conjunction with a list:

```
NoRouteIPs = "{ 127.0.0.0/8, 192.168.0.0/16, \
    172.16.0.0/12, 10.0.0.0/8 }"
ExtIF = "tl0"
block in  quick on $ExtIF from $NoRouteIPs to any
block out quick on $ExtIF from any to $NoRouteIPs
```

Note that macros and lists simplify the pf.conf file, but the lines are actually expanded by pfctl(8) into multiple rules. So, the above example actually expands to the following rules:

```
block in  quick on tl0 inet from 127.0.0.0/8 to any
block in  quick on tl0 inet from 192.168.0.0/16 to any
block in  quick on tl0 inet from 172.16.0.0/12 to any
block in  quick on tl0 inet from 10.0.0.0/8 to any
block out quick on tl0 inet from any to 10.0.0.0/8
block out quick on tl0 inet from any to 172.16.0.0/12
block out quick on tl0 inet from any to 192.168.0.0/16
block out quick on tl0 inet from any to 127.0.0.0/8
```

As you can see, the PF expansion is purely a convenience for the writer and maintainer of the pf.conf file, not an actual simplification of the rules processed by pf(4).

Macros can be used to define more than just addresses and ports; they can be used anywhere in a PF rules file:

```
pre = "pass in quick on ep0 inet proto tcp from "
post = "to any port { 80, 6667 } keep state"
# David's classroom
$pre 21.14.24.80 $post
# Nick's home
$pre 24.2.74.79 $post
$pre 24.2.74.178 $post
```

Expands to:

```
pass in quick on ep0 inet proto tcp from 21.14.24.80 \
    to any port = 80 keep state
pass in quick on ep0 inet proto tcp from 21.14.24.80 \
```

23

```
   to any port = 6667 keep state
pass in quick on ep0 inet proto tcp from 24.2.74.79 \
   to any port = 80 keep state
pass in quick on ep0 inet proto tcp from 24.2.74.79 \
   to any port = 6667 keep state
pass in quick on ep0 inet proto tcp from 24.2.74.178 \
   to any port = 80 keep state
pass in quick on ep0 inet proto tcp from 24.2.74.178 \
   to any port = 6667 keep state
```

5. Tables

5.1. Overview

A table is used to hold a group of IPv4 and/or IPv6 addresses.[1]
Lookups against a table are very fast and consume less memory and
processor time than lists. For this reason, a table is ideal for holding a
large group of addresses as the lookup time on a table holding 50,000
addresses is only slightly more than for one holding 50 addresses. Tables can be used in the following ways:

- source and/or destination address in filter, scrub, NAT, and redirection rules.

- translation address in NAT rules.

- redirection address in redirection rules.

- destination address in route-to, reply-to, and dup-to filter rule
  options.

Tables are created either in pf.conf or by using pfctl(8).

5.2. Configuration

In pf.conf, tables are created using the table directive. The following
attributes may be specified for each table:

- const - the contents of the table cannot be changed once the
  table is created. When this attribute is not specified, pfctl(8)
  may be used to add or remove addresses from the table at any
  time, even when running with a kernel security level of two or
  greater.

---

[1]Note: Tables can not be used to hold port numbers or interface names.

- `persist` - causes the kernel to keep the table in memory even when no rules refer to it. Without this attribute, the kernel will automatically remove the table when the last rule referencing it is flushed.

Note that table names are always enclosed within left angle (<) and right angle bracket characters (>).

In the following example, three tables are created:

```
table <goodguys> { 192.0.2.0/24 }
table <rfc1918> const { 192.168.0.0/16, \
    172.16.0.0/12, 10.0.0.0/8 }
table <spammers> persist
block in on fxp0 from { <rfc1918>, <spammers> } to any
pass  in on fxp0 from <goodguys> to any
```

Addresses can also be specified using the negation (or "not") modifier (!) such as:

```
table <goodguys> { 192.0.2.0/24, !192.0.2.5 }
```

The goodguys table will now match all addresses in the 192.0.2.0/24 network except for 192.0.2.5.

Tables can also be populated from text files containing a list of IP addresses and networks:

```
table <spammers> persist file "/etc/spammers"
block in on fxp0 from <spammers> to any
```

The /etc/spammers file would contain a list of IP addresses and/or CIDR networks, one per line. Any line beginning with a pound character (#) is treated as a comment and ignored.

For another anti-spam technique, see chapter 19 about spamd.

5.3. Manipulating Tables with pfctl

Tables can be manipulated on the fly by using pfctl(8). For instance, to add entries to the <spammers> table created above:

```
# pfctl -t spammers -T add 218.70.0.0/16
```

This will also create the <spammers> table if it doesn't already exist.
To replace the current table definitions from the file use:[2]

```
# pfctl -t spammers -T replace -f /etc/spammers
```

To list the addresses in a table:

```
# pfctl -t spammers -T show
```

The -v argument can also be used with "-Tshow" to display statistics
for each table entry. To remove addresses from a table:

```
# pfctl -t spammers -T delete 218.70.0.0/16
```

And to list the tables known to PF:

```
# pfctl -s Tables
```

For more information on manipulating tables with pfctl, please read
the pfctl(8) manual page.

5.4. Specifying Addresses

In addition to being specified by an IP address, hosts may also be
specified by their hostname. When the hostname is resolved to an
IP address, all resulting IPv4 and IPv6 addresses are placed into the
table. IP addresses can also be entered into a table by specifying a
valid interface name and the table will then contain all IP addresses
assigned to that interface. Or the self keyword can be used and the
table will contain all the IP addresses assigned to the machine (including loopback addresses).

One limitation when specifying addresses is that 0.0.0.0/0 and 0/0
will not work in tables. The alternative is to hard code that address or
use a macro.

---

[2]Reloading the ruleset will also reload the table.

5.5. Address Matching

An address lookup against a table will return the most narrowly matching entry. This allows for the creation of tables such as:

```
table <goodguys> { 172.16.0.0/16, !172.16.1.0/24, \
    172.16.1.100 }
block in on dc0 all
pass  in on dc0 from <goodguys> to any
```

Any packet coming in through dc0 will have its source address matched against the table <goodguys>:

- 172.16.50.5 - narrowest match is 172.16.0.0/16; packet matches the table and will be passed.

- 172.16.1.25 - narrowest match is !172.16.1.0/24; packet matches an entry in the table but that entry is negated (with the "!" modifier); packet does not match the table and will be blocked.

- 172.16.1.100 - exactly matches 172.16.1.100; packet matches the table and will be passed.

- 10.1.4.55 - does not match the table and will be blocked.

6. Packet Filtering

6.1. Overview

Packet filtering is the selective passing or blocking of data packets as they pass through a network interface. The criteria that pf(4) uses when inspecting packets are based on the Layer 3 (IPv4 and IPv6) and Layer 4 (TCP, UDP, ICMP, and ICMPv6) headers. The most often used criteria are source and destination address, source and destination port, and protocol – as introduced in chapter 3.

Filter rules specify the criteria that a packet must match and the resulting action, either `block` or `pass`, that is taken when a match is found. Filter rules are evaluated in sequential order, first to last. Unless the packet matches a rule containing the quick keyword, the packet will be evaluated against *all* filter rules before the final action is taken. The last rule to match is the "winner" and will dictate what action to take on the packet. There is an implicit `pass all` at the beginning of a filtering ruleset meaning that if a packet does not match any filter rule the resulting action will be pass.

6.2. Rule Syntax

The general, *highly simplified* syntax for filter rules is:

```
action [direction] [log] [quick] [on interface] \
  [af] [proto protocol] \
  [from src_addr [port src_port]] \
  [to dst_addr [port dst_port]] \
  [flags tcp_flags] [state]
```

action The action to be taken for matching packets, either `pass` or `block`. The `pass` action will pass the packet back to the kernel for further processing while the `block` action will react based on the setting of the `block-policy` option.[1] The default reaction may be overridden by specifying either `block drop` or `block return`.

direction The direction the packet is moving on an interface, either `in` or `out`.

log Specifies that the packet should be logged via pflogd(8). If the rule specifies the `keep state`, `modulate state`, or `synproxy state` option, then only the packet which establishes the state is logged. To log all packets regardless, use `log (all)`[2]. See the logging chapter on page 111 for more information.

quick If a packet matches a rule specifying `quick`, then that rule is considered the last matching rule and the specified *action* is taken.

interface The name or group of the network interface that the packet is moving through. An interface group is specified as the name of the interface but without the integer appended. For example: ppp or fxp. This would cause the rule to match for any packet traversing any ppp or fxp interface, respectively.

af The address family of the packet, either `inet` for IPv4 or `inet6` for IPv6. PF is usually able to automatically determine this parameter based on the source and/or destination address(es).

protocol The Layer 4 protocol of the packet. See section 3.4 for details on specifying the protocol.

src_addr , **dst_addr** The source/destination address in the IP header. See sections 3.2 and 5.4 for information on how to specify addresses.

src_port , **dst_port** The source/destination port in the Layer 4 packet header. See section 3.3 for information on how to specify ports.

---

[1]For details, see page 65.
[2]Use "`log-all`" instead for versions of PF before 3.8.

tcp_flags Specifies the flags that must be set in the TCP header when using `proto tcp`. Flags are specified as flags `check/mask`. For example: `flags S/SA` - this instructs PF to only look at the S and A (SYN and ACK) flags and to match if only the SYN flag is "on". This is covered further in section 6.10.

state Specifies whether state information is kept on packets matching this rule. (These states are covered in section 6.6.)

- `keep state` - works with TCP, UDP, and ICMP.
- `modulate state` - works only with TCP. PF will generate strong Initial Sequence Numbers (ISNs) for packets matching this rule.
- `synproxy state` - proxies incoming TCP connections to help protect servers from spoofed TCP SYN floods. This option includes the functionality of `keep state` and `modulate state`.

6.3. Default Deny

The recommended practice when setting up a firewall is to take a "default deny" approach. That is, to deny *everything* and then selectively allow certain traffic through the firewall. This approach is recommended because it errs on the side of caution and also makes writing a ruleset easier.

To create a default deny filter policy, the first two filter rules should be:

```
block in  all
block out all
```

This will block all traffic on all interfaces in either direction from anywhere to anywhere.

6.4. Passing Traffic

Traffic must now be explicitly passed through the firewall or it will be dropped by the default deny policy (as created above). This is where packet criteria such as source/destination port, source/destination address, and protocol come into play. Whenever traffic is permitted to pass through the firewall the rule(s) should be written to be as restrictive as possible. This is to ensure that the intended traffic, and only the intended traffic, is permitted to pass.

Some examples:

```
# Pass traffic in on dc0 from the local network,
# 192.168.0.0/24, to the BSD machine's IP address
# 192.168.0.1. Also, pass the return traffic out
# on dc0.
pass in  on dc0 from 192.168.0.0/24 to 192.168.0.1
pass out on dc0 from 192.168.0.1 to 192.168.0.0/24

# Pass TCP traffic in on fxp0 to the web server
# running on the BSD machine. The interface name,
# fxp0, is used as the destination address so that
# packets will only match this rule if they are
# destined for the BSD machine.
pass in on fxp0 proto tcp from any to fxp0 port www
```

6.5. The quick Keyword

As indicated earlier, each packet is evaluated against the filter ruleset from top to bottom. By default, the packet is marked for passage, which can be changed by any rule, and could be changed back and forth several times before the end of the filter rules. **The last matching rule "wins".** There is an exception to this: The quick option on a filtering rule has the effect of canceling any further rule processing and causes the specified action to be taken. Let's look at a couple examples.

Wrong:

```
block in on fxp0 proto tcp from any to any port ssh
pass  in all
```

In this case, the block line may be evaluated, but will never have any effect, as it is then followed by a line which will pass everything.

Better:

```
block in quick on fxp0 proto tcp from any to any port ssh
pass  in all
```

These rules are evaluated a little differently. If the block line is matched, due to the `quick` option, the packet will be blocked, and the rest of the ruleset will be ignored.

6.6. Keeping State

One of Packet Filter's important abilities is "keeping state" or "stateful inspection". Stateful inspection refers to PF's ability to track the state, or progress, of a network connection. By storing information about each connection in a state table, PF is able to quickly determine if a packet passing through the firewall belongs to an already established connection. If it does, it is passed through the firewall without going through ruleset evaluation.

Keeping state has many advantages including simpler rulesets and better packet filtering performance. PF is able to match packets moving in *either* direction to state table entries meaning that filter rules which pass returning traffic don't need to be written. And, since packets matching stateful connections don't go through ruleset evaluation, the time PF spends processing those packets can be greatly lessened.

When a rule has the `keep state` option, the first packet matching the rule creates a "state" between the sender and receiver. Now, not only do packets going from the sender to receiver match the state entry and bypass ruleset evaluation, but so do the reply packets from receiver to sender. For example:

```
pass out on fxp0 proto tcp from any to any keep state
```

This allows any outbound TCP traffic on the fxp0 interface and also permits the reply traffic to pass back through the firewall. While keeping state is a nice feature, its use significantly improves the performance of your firewall as state lookups are dramatically faster than running a packet through the filter rules.

The modulate state option works just like keep state except with modulate state, the Initial Sequence Number (ISN) of outgoing connections is randomized. This is useful for protecting connections initiated by certain operating systems that do a poor job of choosing ISNs. Starting with PF 3.5, the modulate state option can be used in rules that specify protocols other than just TCP.

Keep state on outgoing TCP, UDP, and ICMP packets and modulate TCP ISNs:

```
pass out on fxp0 proto { tcp, udp, icmp } from any \
    to any modulate state
```

Another advantage of keeping state is that corresponding ICMP traffic will be passed through the firewall. For example, if keep state is specified for a TCP connection and an ICMP source-quench message referring to this TCP connection arrives, it will be matched to the appropriate state entry and passed through the firewall.

The scope of a state entry is controlled globally by the state-policy runtime option[3] and on a per rule basis by the if-bound, group-bound, and floating state option keywords. These per rule keywords have the same meaning as when used with the state-policy option. Example:

```
pass out on fxp0 proto { tcp, udp, icmp } from any \
    to any modulate state (if-bound)
```

This rule would dictate that in order for packets to match the state entry, they must be transiting the fxp0 interface.

Note that nat, binat, and rdr[4] rules implicitly create state for matching connections as long as the connection is passed by the filter ruleset.

6.7. Keeping State for UDP

One will sometimes hear it said that, "One can not create state with UDP as UDP is a stateless protocol!" While it is true that a UDP

---

[3] See the Runtime Options chapter 9 for more information.

[4] These are covered in chapters 7 and 8.

communication session does not have any concept of state (an explicit start and stop of communications), this does not have any impact on PF's ability to create state for a UDP session. In the case of protocols without "start" and "end" packets, PF simply keeps track of how long it has been since a matching packet has gone through. If the timeout is reached, the state is cleared. The timeout values can be set in the options section of the pf.conf file.[5]

6.8. TCP SYN Proxy

Normally when a client initiates a TCP connection to a server, PF will pass the handshake packets between the two endpoints as they arrive. PF has the ability, however, to proxy the handshake. With the handshake proxied, PF itself will complete the handshake with the client, initiate a handshake with the server, and then pass packets between the two. The benefit of this process is that no packets are sent to the server before the client completes the handshake. This eliminates the threat of spoofed TCP SYN floods affecting the server because a spoofed client connection will be unable to complete the handshake.

The TCP SYN proxy is enabled using the `synproxy state` keywords in filter rules. Example:

```
pass in on $ext_if proto tcp from any to $web_server \
    port www flags S/SA synproxy state
```

Here, connections to the web server will be TCP proxied by PF.

Because of the way `synproxy state` works, it also includes the same functionality as `keep state` and `modulate state`.

The SYN proxy will not work if PF is running on a bridge(4).

6.9. Stateful Tracking Options

When a filter rule creates a state table entry through the use of any of the `keep state`, `modulate state`, or `synproxy state` keywords,

---

[5]Timeouts are introduced on page 68.

certain options can be specified that control the behavior of state creation. The following options are available[6]:

max *number* Limit the maximum number of state entries the rule can create to *number*. If the maximum is reached, packets that would normally create state are dropped until the number of existing states decreases.

source-track This option enables the tracking of number of states created per source IP address. This option has two formats:

- source-track rule - The maximum number of states created by this rule is limited by the rule's max-src-nodes and max-src-states options. Only state entries created by this particular rule count toward the rule's limits.

- source-track global - The number of states created by all rules that use this option is limited. Each rule can specify different max-src-nodes and max-src-states options, however state entries created by any participating rule count towards each individual rule's limits.

The total number of source IP addresses tracked globally can be controlled via the src-nodes runtime option.

max-src-nodes *number* When the source-track option is used, max-src-nodes will limit the number of source IP addresses that can simultaneously create state. This option can only be used with source-track rule.

max-src-states *number* When the source-track option is used, max-src-states will limit the number of simultaneous state entries that can be created per source IP address. The scope of this limit (i.e., states created by this rule only or states created by all rules that use source-track) is dependent on the source-track option specified.

---

[6]The max-src-states,   max-src-nodes,   max-src-nodes,   and max-src-conn-rate options were added in PF 3.7.

An example rule:

```
pass in on $ext_if proto tcp to $web_server \
    port www flags S/SA keep state \
    (max 200, source-track rule, max-src-nodes 100, \
    max-src-states 3)
```

The rule above defines the following behavior:

- Limit the absolute maximum number of states that this rule can create to 200.

- Enable source tracking; limit state creation based on states created by this rule only.

- Limit the maximum number of source addresses that can simultaneously create state to 100.

- Limit the maximum number of simultaneous states per source IP to 3.

A separate set of restrictions can be placed on stateful TCP connections that have completed the 3-way handshake.

max-src-conn *number* Limit the maximum number of simultaneous TCP connections which have completed the 3-way handshake that a single host can make.

max-src-conn-rate *number / interval* Limit the rate of new connections to a certain amount per time interval.

Both of these options automatically invoke the source-track rule option and are incompatible with source-track global.

Since these limits are only being placed on TCP connections that have completed the 3-way handshake, more aggressive actions can be taken on offending IP addresses.

overload *<table>* Put an offending host's IP address into the named table.

flush [global] Kill any other states that match this rule and
that were created by this source IP. When global[7] is specified,
kill all states matching this source IP, regardless of which rule
created the state.

An example:

```
table <abusive_hosts> persist
block in quick from <abusive_hosts>

pass in on $ext_if proto tcp to $web_server \
    port www flags S/SA keep state \
    (max-src-conn 100, max-src-conn-rate 15/5, \
    overload <abusive_hosts> flush)
```

This does the following:

- Limits the maximum number of connections per source to 100

- Rate limits the number of connections to 15 in a 5 second span

- Puts the IP address of any host that breaks these limits into the
  <abusive_hosts> table

- For any offending IP addresses, flush any states created by this
  rule.

6.10. TCP Flags

Matching TCP packets based on flags is most often used to filter TCP
packets that are attempting to open a new connection. The TCP flags
and their meanings are listed here:

- **F** : FIN - Finish; end of session

- **S** : SYN - Synchronize; indicates request to start session

- **R** : RST - Reset; drop a connection

---

[7]The global modifier was added in PF 3.7.

- **P** : PUSH - Push; packet is sent immediately

- **A** : ACK - Acknowledgement

- **U** : URG - Urgent

- **E** : ECE - Explicit Congestion Notification Echo

- **W** : CWR - Congestion Window Reduced

To have PF inspect the TCP flags during evaluation of a rule, the
flags keyword is used with the following syntax:

```
flags check/mask
```

The *mask* part tells PF to only inspect the specified flags and the *check*
part specifies which flag(s) must be "on" in the header for a match to
occur. A mask must be specified.

```
pass in on fxp0 proto tcp from any to any port ssh \
    flags S/SA
```

The above rule passes TCP traffic with the SYN flag set while only
looking at the SYN and ACK flags. A packet with the SYN and ECE
flags would match the above rule while a packet with SYN and ACK
or just ACK would not.

Flags are often used in conjunction with keep state rules to help
control the creation of state entries:

```
pass out on fxp0 proto tcp all flags S/SA keep state
```

This would permit the creation of state on any outgoing TCP packet
with the SYN flag set out of the SYN and ACK flags.

One should be careful with using flags – understand what you are
doing and why, and be careful with the advice people give as a lot of
it is bad. Some people have suggested creating state "only if the SYN
flag is set and no others". Such a bad idea would end with this:

```
. . . flags S/FSRPAUEW
```

The theory is, create state only on the start of the TCP session, and the session should start with a SYN flag, and no others. The problem is some sites are starting to use the ECN flag and any site using ECN that tries to connect to you would be rejected by such a rule. A much better guideline is:

```
. . . flags S/SAFR
```

While this is practical and safe, it is also unnecessary to check the FIN and RST flags if traffic is also being scrubbed. The scrubbing process will cause PF to drop any incoming packets with illegal TCP flag combinations (such as SYN and RST) and to normalize potentially ambiguous combinations (such as SYN and FIN). It's highly recommended to always scrub incoming traffic:

```
scrub in on fxp0
.
.
.
pass in on fxp0 proto tcp from any to any port ssh \
    flags S/SA keep state
```

Scrubbing is covered in more detail in chapter 10.

6.11. Blocking Spoofed Packets

Address "spoofing" is when an malicious user fakes the source IP address in packets they transmit in order to either hide their real address or to impersonate another node on the network. Once the user has spoofed their address they can launch a network attack without revealing the true source of the attack or attempt to gain access to network services that are restricted to certain IP addresses.

PF offers some protection against address spoofing through the antispoof keyword:

```
antispoof [log] [quick] for interface [af]
```

log Specifies that matching packets should be logged via pflogd(8).

quick If a packet matches this rule then it will be considered the "winning" rule and ruleset evaluation will stop.

interface The network interface to activate spoofing protection on. This can also be a list of interfaces.

af The address family to activate spoofing protection for, either inet for IPv4 or inet6 for IPv6.

Example:

```
antispoof for fxp0 inet
```

When a ruleset is loaded, any occurrences of the antispoof keyword are expanded into two filter rules. Assuming that interface fxp0 has IP address 10.0.0.1 and a subnet mask of 255.255.255.0 (i.e., a /24), the above antispoof rule would expand to:

```
block in on ! fxp0 inet from 10.0.0.0/24 to any
block in inet from 10.0.0.1 to any
```

These rules accomplish two things:

- Blocks all traffic coming from the 10.0.0.0/24 network that does *not* pass in through fxp0. Since the 10.0.0.0/24 network is on the fxp0 interface, packets with a source address in that network block should never be seen coming in on any other interface.

- Blocks all incoming traffic from 10.0.0.1, the IP address on fxp0. The host machine should never send packets to itself through an external interface, so any incoming packets with a source address belonging to the machine can be considered malicious.

Note: The filter rules that the antispoof rule expands to will also block packets sent over the loopback interface to local addresses. It's best practice to skip filtering on loopback interfaces anyways, but this becomes a necessity when using antispoof rules:

```
set skip on lo0
antispoof for fxp0 inet
```

Usage of antispoof should be restricted to interfaces that have been assigned an IP address. Using antispoof on an interface without an IP address will result in filter rules such as:

```
block drop in on ! fxp0 inet all
block drop in inet all
```

With these rules there is a risk of blocking *all* inbound traffic on *all* interfaces.

6.12. Shortcuts for Creating Rulesets

Packet Filter's grammar is quite flexible which, in turn, allows for great flexibility in a ruleset. PF is able to infer certain keywords which means that they don't have to be explicitly stated in a rule, and keyword ordering is relaxed such that it isn't necessary to memorize strict syntax.

Elimination of Keywords

To define a "default deny" policy, two rules are used (as shown in section 6.3):

```
block in  all
block out all
```

This can be reduced to:

```
block all
```

When no direction is specified, PF will assume the rule applies to packets moving in both directions.

Similarly, the "from any to any" and "all" clauses can be left out of a rule, for example:

```
block in on rl0 all
pass  in quick log on rl0 proto tcp from any to any \
  port 22 keep state
```

can be simplified as:

```
block in on rl0
pass in quick log on rl0 proto tcp to port 22 keep state
```

The first rule blocks all incoming packets from anywhere to anywhere on rl0, and the second rule passes in TCP traffic on rl0 to port 22.

Return Simplification

A ruleset used to block packets and reply with a TCP RST or ICMP Unreachable response could look like this:

```
block in all
block return-rst in proto tcp all
block return-icmp in proto udp all
block out all
block return-rst out proto tcp all
block return-icmp out proto udp all
```

This can be simplified as:

```
block return
```

When PF sees the return keyword, it's smart enough to send the proper response, or no response at all, depending on the protocol of the packet being blocked.

Keyword Ordering

The order in which keywords are specified is flexible in most cases. For example, a rule written as:

```
pass in log quick on rl0 proto tcp to port 22 \
  flags S/SA keep state queue ssh label ssh
```

Can also be written as:

```
pass in quick log on rl0 proto tcp to port 22 \
   queue ssh keep state label ssh flags S/SA
```

Other, similar variations will also work.

6.13. Passive Operating System Fingerprinting

Passive OS Fingerprinting (OSFP) is a method for passively detecting the operating system of a remote host based on certain characteristics within that host's TCP SYN packets. This information can then be used as criteria within filter rules.

PF determines the remote operating system by comparing characteristics of a TCP SYN packet against the fingerprints file, which by default is /etc/pf.os.[8]Once PF is enabled, the current fingerprint list can be viewed with this command:

```
# pfctl -s osfp
```

Within a filter rule, a fingerprint may be specified by OS class, version, or subtype/patch level. Each of these items is listed in the output of the pfctl command shown above. To specify a fingerprint in a filter rule, the os keyword is used:

```
pass  in on $ext_if from any os OpenBSD keep state
block in on $ext_if from any os "Windows 2000"
block in on $ext_if from any os "Linux 2.4 ts"
block in on $ext_if from any os unknown
```

The special operating system class unknown allows for matching packets when the OS fingerprint is not known.

Take note of the following:

---

[8]To select a different operating system fingerprints file, use the set fingerprints option described in the Runtime Options chapter 9. Also, OpenBSD's version of tcpdump has an option for OSFP using the same /etc/pf.os.

- Operating system fingerprints are occasionally wrong due to spoofed and/or crafted packets that are made to look like they originated from a specific operating system.

- Certain revisions or patchlevels of an operating system may change the stack's behavior and cause it to either not match what's in the fingerprints file or to match another entry altogether.

- OSFP only works on the TCP SYN packet; it will not work on other protocols or on already established connections.

This is based on Michal Zalewski's p0f (passive OS fingerprinting) code. Signatures can be contributed via the p0f fingerprint submission webpage at http://lcamtuf.coredump.cx/p0f-help/.

6.14. IP Options

By default, PF blocks packets with IP options set (such as the RECORD_ROUTE option used by ping -R). This can make the job more difficult for "OS fingerprinting" utilities like nmap. IP options are rarely used and are not required for proper IP operation. Details can be found in RFC 791, "Internet Protocol", and RFC 1108, "Security Options for the Internet Protocol".

If you have an application that requires the passing of these packets, such as multicast or IGMP, you can use the allow-opts directive with pass rules:

```
pass in quick on fxp0 all allow-opts
```

Or this can be specific for IGMP, for example:

```
pass in proto igmp all allow-opts
pass out proto igmp all allow-opts
```

6.15. Filtering Ruleset Example

Below is an example of a filtering ruleset. The machine running PF is acting as a firewall between a small, internal network and the Internet. Only the filter rules are shown; queueing, nat, rdr, etc., have been left out of this example.

```
ext_if = "fxp0"
int_if  = "dc0"
lan_net = "192.168.0.0/24"

# Table containing all IP addresses assigned to
# the firewall.
table <firewall> const { self }

# Don't filter on the loopback interface.
set skip on lo0

# Scrub incoming packets.
scrub in all

# Setup a default deny policy
block all

# Activate spoofing protection for the
# internal interface.
antispoof quick for $int_if inet

# Only allow ssh connections from the local network
# if it's from the trusted computer, 192.168.0.15.
# Use "block return" so that a TCP RST is sent to
# close blocked connections right away. Use "quick"
# so that this rule is not overridden by the "pass"
# rules below.
block return in quick on $int_if proto tcp \
    from ! 192.168.0.15 \
    to $int_if port ssh flags S/SA
```

```
# Pass all traffic to and from the local network.
pass in  on $int_if from $lan_net to any
pass out on $int_if from any to $lan_net

# Pass tcp, udp, and icmp out on the external
# (Internet) interface.
# Keep state on udp and icmp and modulate state on tcp.
pass out on $ext_if proto tcp all \
   modulate state flags S/SA
pass out on $ext_if proto { udp, icmp } all keep state

# Allow ssh connections in on the external interface
# as long as they're NOT destined for the firewall
# (i.e., they're destined for a machine on the local
# network). Log the initial packet so that we can
# later tell who is trying to connect. Use the tcp syn
# proxy to proxy the connection.
pass in log on $ext_if proto tcp from any \
  to ! <firewall> \
  port ssh flags S/SA synproxy state
```

7. Network Address Translation

7.1. Overview

Network Address Translation (NAT) is a way to map an entire network (or networks) to a single IP address. NAT is necessary when the number of IP addresses assigned to you by your Internet Service Provider is less than the total number of computers that you wish to provide Internet access for. NAT is described in RFC 1631,"The IP Network Address Translator (NAT)."[1]

NAT allows you to take advantage of the reserved address blocks described in RFC 1918, "Address Allocation for Private Internets."[2] Typically, your internal network will be setup to use one or more of these network blocks. They are:

10.0.0.0/8 (10.0.0.0 - 10.255.255.255)

172.16.0.0/12 (172.16.0.0 - 172.31.255.255)

192.168.0.0/16 (192.168.0.0 - 192.168.255.255)

A system doing NAT will have at least two network adapters, one to the Internet, the other to your internal network. NAT will be translating requests from the internal network so they appear to all be coming from your NAT system.

7.2. How NAT Works

When a client on the internal network contacts a machine on the Internet, it sends out IP packets destined for that machine. These packets

---

[1] http://www.ietf.org/rfc/rfc1631.txt
[2] http://www.ietf.org/rfc/rfc1918.txt

contain all the addressing information necessary to get them to their destination. NAT is concerned with these pieces of information:

- Source IP address (for example, 192.168.1.35)

- Source TCP or UDP port (for example, 2132)

When the packets pass through the NAT gateway they will be modified so that they appear to be coming from the NAT gateway itself. The NAT gateway will record the changes it makes in its state table so that it can reverse the changes on return packets and ensure that return packets are passed through the firewall and are not blocked. For example, the following changes might be made:

- Source IP: replaced with the external address of the gateway (for example, 24.5.0.5)

- Source port: replaced with a randomly chosen, unused port on the gateway (for example, 53136)

Neither the internal machine nor the Internet host is aware of these translation steps. To the internal machine, the NAT system is simply an Internet gateway. To the Internet host, the packets appear to come directly from the NAT system; it is completely unaware that the internal workstation even exists.

When the Internet host replies to the internal machine's packets, they will be addressed to the NAT gateway's external IP (24.5.0.5) at the translation port (53136). The NAT gateway will then search the state table to determine if the reply packets match an already established connection. A unique match will be found based on the IP/port combination which tells PF the packets belong to a connection initiated by the internal machine 192.168.1.35. PF will then make the opposite changes it made to the outgoing packets and forward the reply packets on to the internal machine.

Translation of ICMP packets happens in a similar fashion but without the source port modification.

7.3. NAT and Packet Filtering

Translated packets must still pass through the filter engine and will be blocked or passed based on the filter rules that have been defined. The *only* exception to this rule is when the `pass` keyword is used within the `nat` rule. This will cause the NATed packets to pass right through the filtering engine.

Also be aware that since translation occurs *before* filtering, the filter engine will see the *translated* packet with the translated IP address and port as outlined in the previous section 7.2.

7.4. IP Forwarding

Since NAT is almost always used on routers and network gateways, it will probably be necessary to enable IP forwarding so that packets can travel between network interfaces on the BSD machine. IP forwarding is enabled using the sysctl(3) mechanism:

```
# sysctl -w net.inet.ip.forwarding=1
# sysctl -w net.inet6.ip6.forwarding=1 (if using IPv6)
```

To make this change permanent, the following lines should be added to /etc/sysctl.conf:

```
net.inet.ip.forwarding=1
net.inet6.ip6.forwarding=1
```

On OpenBSD, these lines are present but commented out (prefixed with a #) in the default install. Remove the # and save the file. IP forwarding will be enabled when the machine is rebooted.

Or on DragonFly and FreeBSD, this can also be done by setting the following in your /etc/rc.conf file:

```
gateway_enable=YES
ipv6_gateway_enable=YES
```

7.5. Configuring NAT

The general format for NAT rules in pf.conf looks something like this:

```
nat [pass [log]] on interface [af] \
    from src_addr [port src_port] \
    to dst_addr [port dst_port] \
    -> ext_addr [pool_type] [static-port]
```

nat The keyword that begins a NAT rule.

pass Causes translated packets to completely bypass the filter rules.

log When pass is specified, packets can be logged via pflogd(8). Normally only the first packet that matches will be logged. To log all matching packets, use log (all)[3]. See chapter 15 for logging information.

interface The name of the network interface to translate packets on.

af The address family, either inet for IPv4 or inet6 for IPv6. PF is usually able to determine this parameter based on the source or destination address(es).

src_addr The source (internal) address of packets that will be translated. See sections 3.2 and 5.4 for information on how to specify addresses.

src_port The source port in the Layer 4 packet header. The port option is not usually used in nat rules because the goal is usually to NAT all traffic regardless of the port(s) being used. (If needed, see section 3.3 for information on how to specify ports.)

dst_addr The destination address of packets to be translated. The destination address is specified in the same way as the source address.

dst_port The destination port in the Layer 4 packet header. This port is specified in the same way as the source port.

---

[3]The "log (all)" feature was added for nat/rdr/binat pass rules in PF 3.8.

ext_addr The external (translation) address on the NAT gateway that packets will be translated to. The destination address is specified in the same way as the source address.

pool_type Specifies the type of address pool to use for translation. This is covered in chapter 13.

`static-port` Tells PF not to translate the source port in TCP and UDP packets.

This would lead to a most basic form of this line similar to this:

```
nat on tl0 from 192.168.1.0/24 to any -> 24.5.0.5
```

This rule says to perform NAT on the tl0 interface for any packets coming from 192.168.1.0/24 and to replace the source IP address with 24.5.0.5.

While the above rule is correct, it is not recommended form. Maintenance could be difficult as any change of the external or internal network numbers would require the line be changed. Compare instead with this easier to maintain line (tl0 is external, dc0 internal):

```
nat on tl0 from dc0:network to any -> tl0
```

The advantage should be fairly clear: you can change the IP addresses of either interface without changing this rule.

When specifying an interface name for the translation address as above, the IP address is determined at pf.conf *load* time, not on the fly. If you are using DHCP to configure your external interface, this can be a problem. If your assigned IP address changes, NAT will continue translating outgoing packets using the old IP address. This will cause outgoing connections to stop functioning. To get around this, you can tell PF to automatically update the translation address by putting parentheses around the interface name:

```
nat on tl0 from dc0:network to any -> (tl0)
```

This method works for translation to both IPv4 and IPv6 addresses.

7.6. Bidirectional Mapping (1:1 mapping)

A bidirectional mapping can be established by using the `binat` rule. A binat rule establishes a one to one mapping between an internal IP address and an external address. This can be useful, for example, to provide a web server on the internal network with its own external IP address. Connections from the Internet to the external address will be translated to the internal address and connections from the web server (such as DNS requests) will be translated to the external address. TCP and UDP ports are never modified with `binat` rules as they are with nat rules.

Example:

```
web_serv_int = "192.168.1.100"
web_serv_ext = "24.5.0.6"
binat on tl0 from $web_serv_int to any -> $web_serv_ext
```

7.7. Translation Rule Exceptions

Exceptions can be made to translation rules by using the no keyword. For example, if the NAT example above was modified to look like this:

```
no nat on tl0 from 192.168.1.208 to any
nat on tl0 from 192.168.1.0/24 to any -> 24.2.74.79
```

Then the entire 192.168.1.0/24 network would have its packets translated to the external address 24.2.74.79 except for 192.168.1.208.

Note that the first matching rule wins; if it's a no rule, then the packet is not translated. The no keyword can also be used with binat and rdr rules.

7.8. Checking NAT Status

To view the active NAT translations, pfctl(8) is used with the -s state option. This command will list all the current NAT sessions, for example:

```
# pfctl -s state
fxp0 TCP 192.168.1.35:2132 -> 24.5.0.5:53136 -> \
   65.42.33.245:22 TIME_WAIT:TIME_WAIT
fxp0 UDP 192.168.1.35:2491 -> 24.5.0.5:60527 -> \
   24.2.68.33:53 MULTIPLE:SINGLE
```

Explanations (first line only):

fxp0 Indicates the interface that the state is bound to. The word "self" will appear if the state is floating.

TCP The protocol being used by the connection.

192.168.1.35:2132 The IP address (192.168.1.35) of the machine on the internal network. The source port (2132) is shown after the address. This is also the address that is replaced in the IP header.

24.5.0.5:53136 The IP address (24.5.0.5) and port (53136) on the gateway that packets are being translated to.

65.42.33.245:22 The IP address (65.42.33.245) and the port (22) that the internal machine is connecting to.

TIME_WAIT:TIME_WAIT This indicates the source and destination states that PF believes the connection to be in.

8. Traffic Redirection (Port Forwarding)

8.1. Overview

When you have NAT running in your office you have the entire Internet available to all your machines. What if you have a machine behind the NAT gateway that needs to be accessed from outside? This is where redirection comes in. Redirection allows incoming traffic to be sent to a machine behind the NAT gateway. (Using redirection to implement load balancing is covered in chapter 13.)

8.2. Redirection Example

Let's look at an example:

```
rdr on tl0 proto tcp from any to any port 80 \
   -> 192.168.1.20
```

This line redirects TCP port 80 (web server) traffic to a machine inside the network at 192.168.1.20. So, even though 192.168.1.20 is behind your gateway and inside your network, the outside world can access it.

The from any to any part of the above rdr line can be quite useful. If you know what addresses or subnets are supposed to have access to the web server at port 80, you can restrict them here:

```
rdr on tl0 proto tcp from 27.146.49.0/24 to any \
   port 80 -> 192.168.1.20
```

This will redirect only the specified subnet. Note this implies you can redirect different incoming hosts to different machines behind the gateway. This can be quite useful. For example, you could have users at remote sites access their own desktop computers using the same port and IP address on the gateway as long as you know the IP address they will be connecting from:

```
rdr on tl0 proto tcp from 27.146.49.14 to any \
    port 80 -> 192.168.1.20
rdr on tl0 proto tcp from 16.114.4.89 to any \
    port 80 -> 192.168.1.22
rdr on tl0 proto tcp from 24.2.74.178 to any \
    port 80 -> 192.168.1.23
```

A range of ports can also be redirected within the same rule:

```
rdr on tl0 proto tcp from any to any \
    port 5000:5500 -> 192.168.1.20
rdr on tl0 proto tcp from any to any \
    port 5000:5500 -> 192.168.1.20 port 6000
rdr on tl0 proto tcp from any to any \
    port 5000:5500 -> 192.168.1.20 port 7000:*
```

These examples show ports 5000 to 5500 inclusive being redirected to 192.168.1.20. In this first rule, port 5000 is redirected to 5000, 5001 to 5001, etc. In the second rule, the entire port range is redirected to port 6000. And in third rule, port 5000 is redirected to 7000, 5001 to 7001, etc.

8.3. Redirection and Packet Filtering

Translated packets must still pass through the filter engine and will be blocked or passed based on the filter rules that have been defined.

The *only* exception to this rule is when the pass keyword is used within the rdr rule. In this case, the redirected packets will pass statefully right through the filtering engine: the filter rules won't be evaluated against these packets. This is a handy shortcut to avoid adding pass filter rules for each redirection rule. Think of it as a normal rdr rule (with no pass keyword) associated to a pass filter rule with the `keep state` keyword. However, if you want to enable more specific filtering options such as `synproxy state`, `modulate state`, etc. you'll still have to use a dedicated `pass` rule as these options don't fit into redirection rules.

Also be aware that since translation occurs *before* filtering, the filter engine will see the *translated* packet as it looks after it has had its destination IP address and/or destination port changed to match the redirection address/port specified in the `rdr` rule. Consider this scenario:

- 192.0.2.1 - host on the Internet

- 24.65.1.13 - external address of BSD router

- 192.168.1.5 - internal IP address of web server

Redirection rule:

```
rdr on tl0 proto tcp from 192.0.2.1 to 24.65.1.13 \
    port 80 -> 192.168.1.5 port 8000
```

Packet before the `rdr` rule is processed:

- Source address: 192.0.2.1

- Source port: 4028 (arbitrarily chosen by the operating system)

- Destination address: 24.65.1.13

- Destination port: 80

Packet after the `rdr` rule is processed:

- Source address: 192.0.2.1

- Source port: 4028

- Destination address: 192.168.1.5

- Destination port: 8000

The filter engine will see the IP packet as it looks after translation has taken place.

8.4. Security Implications

Redirection does have security implications. Punching a hole in the firewall to allow traffic into the internal, protected network potentially opens up the internal machine to compromise. If traffic is forwarded to an internal web server for example, and a vulnerability is discovered in the web server daemon or in a CGI script run on the web server, then that machine can be compromised from an intruder on the Internet. From there, the intruder has a doorway to the internal network, one that is permitted to pass right through the firewall.

These risks can be minimized by keeping the externally accessed system tightly confined on a separate network. This network is often referred to as a Demilitarized Zone (DMZ) or a Private Service Network (PSN). This way, if the web server is compromised, the effects can be limited to the DMZ/PSN network by careful filtering of the traffic permitted to and from the DMZ/PSN.

8.5. Redirection and Reflection

Often, redirection rules are used to forward incoming connections from the Internet to a local server with a private address in the internal network or LAN, as in:

```
server = 192.168.1.40
rdr on $ext_if proto tcp from any to $ext_if \
   port 80 -> $server port 80
```

But when the redirection rule is tested from a client on the LAN, it doesn't work. The reason is that redirection rules apply only to packets that pass through the specified interface ($ext_if, the external interface, in the example). Connecting to the external address of the firewall from a host on the LAN, however, does not mean the packets will actually pass through its external interface. The TCP/IP stack on the firewall compares the destination address of incoming packets with its own addresses and aliases and detects connections to itself as soon as they have passed the internal interface. Such packets do not physically pass through the external interface, and the stack does not simulate such a passage in any way. Thus, PF never sees these packets on the external interface, and the redirection rule, specifying the external interface, does not apply.

Adding a second redirection rule for the internal interface does not have the desired effect either. When the local client connects to the external address of the firewall, the initial packet of the TCP handshake reaches the firewall through the internal interface. The redirection rule does apply and the destination address gets replaced with that of the internal server. The packet gets forwarded back through the internal interface and reaches the internal server. But the source address has not been translated, and still contains the local client's address, so the server sends its replies directly to the client. The firewall never sees the reply and has no chance to properly reverse the translation. The client receives a reply from a source it never expected and drops it. The TCP handshake then fails and no connection can be established.

Still, it's often desirable for clients on the LAN to connect to the same internal server as external clients and to do so transparently. There are several solutions for this problem:

Split-Horizon DNS

It's possible to configure DNS servers to answer queries from local hosts differently than external queries so that local clients will receive the internal server's address during name resolution. They will then connect directly to the local server, and the firewall isn't involved at all. This reduces local traffic since packets don't have to be sent through the firewall.

Moving the Server Into a Separate Local Network

Adding an additional network interface to the firewall and moving the local server from the client's network into a dedicated network (DMZ) allows redirecting of connections from local clients in the same way as the redirection of external connections. Use of separate networks has several advantages, including improving security by isolating the server from the remaining local hosts. Should the server (which in our case is reachable from the Internet) ever become compromised, it can't access other local hosts directly as all connections have to pass through the firewall.

TCP Proxying

A generic TCP proxy can be setup on the firewall, either listening on the port to be forwarded or getting connections on the internal interface redirected to the port it's listening on. When a local client connects to the firewall, the proxy accepts the connection, establishes a second connection to the internal server, and forwards data between those two connections.

Simple proxies can be created using inetd(8) and netcat.[1] The following /etc/inetd.conf entry creates a listening socket bound to the loopback address (127.0.0.1) and port 5000. Connections are forwarded to port 80 on server 192.168.1.10.

```
127.0.0.1:5000 stream tcp nowait nobody /usr/bin/nc \
    nc -w 20 192.168.1.10 80
```

The following redirection rule forwards port 80 on the internal interface to the proxy:

```
rdr on $int_if proto tcp from $int_net to $ext_if \
    port 80 -> 127.0.0.1 port 5000
```

RDR and NAT Combination

With an additional NAT rule on the internal interface, the lacking source address translation described above can be achieved.

```
rdr on $int_if proto tcp from $int_net to $ext_if \
    port 80 -> $server
no nat on $int_if proto tcp from $int_if \
    to $int_net
nat on $int_if proto tcp from $int_net to $server \
    port 80 -> $int_if
```

---

[1] The nc (aka netcat) utility is included with the default installs of FreeBSD and OpenBSD. For DragonFly and NetBSD, it is available via pkgsrc at net/netcat.

This will cause the initial packet from the client to be translated again when it's forwarded back through the internal interface, replacing the client's source address with the firewall's internal address. The internal server will reply back to the firewall, which can reverse both NAT and RDR translations when forwarding to the local client. This construct is rather complex as it creates two separate states for each reflected connection. Care must be taken to prevent the NAT rule from applying to other traffic, for instance connections originating from external hosts (through other redirections) or the firewall itself. Note that the rdr rule above will cause the TCP/IP stack to see packets arriving on the internal interface with a destination address inside the internal network.

In general, the previously mentioned solutions should be used instead.

9. Runtime Options

9.1. Overview

Options are used to control PF's operation. Options are specified in pf.conf using the `set` directive.

Note: In PF 3.7 and later, the behavior of runtime options has changed. Previously, once an option was set it was never reset to its default value, even if the ruleset was reloaded. Starting in PF 3.7, whenever a ruleset is loaded, the runtime options are reset to default values before the ruleset is parsed. Thus, if an option is set and is then removed from the ruleset and the ruleset reloaded, the option will be reset to its default value.

9.2. The set Command

set block-policy *option* Sets the default behavior for filter rules that specify the `block` action.

- `drop` - packet is silently dropped.
- `return` - a TCP RST packet is returned for blocked TCP packets and an ICMP Unreachable packet is returned for all others.

Note that individual filter rules can override the default response. The default is `drop`.

set debug *option* Set PF's debugging level.

- `none` - no debugging messages are shown.
- `urgent` - debug messages generated for serious errors.

- `misc` - debug messages generated for various errors (e.g., to see status from the packet normalizer/scrubber and for state creation failures).
- `loud` - debug messages generated for common conditions (e.g., to see status from the passive OS fingerprinter).

The default is `urgent`.

set fingerprints *file* Sets the file to load operating system fingerprints from. For use with passive OS fingerprinting which is covered in section 6.13. The default is /etc/pf.os.

set limit *option value* Set various limits on PF's operation.

- `frags` - maximum number of entries in the memory pool used for packet reassembly (scrub rules). Default is 5000.
- `src-nodes` - maximum number of entries in the memory pool used for tracking source IP addresses (generated by the sticky-address and source-track options). Default is 10000.
- `states` - maximum number of entries in the memory pool used for state table entries (filter rules that specify keep state). Default is 10000.

set loginterface *interface* Sets the interface for which PF should gather statistics such as bytes in and out and packets passed and blocked. Statistics can only be gathered for *one* interface at a time. Note that the match, bad-offset, etc., counters and the state table counters are recorded regardless of whether `loginterface` is set or not. To turn this option off, set it to none. The default is none.

set optimization *option* Optimize PF for one of the following network environments:

- `normal` - suitable for almost all networks.

- high-latency - high latency networks such as satellite connections.

- aggressive - aggressively expires connections from the state table. This can greatly reduce the memory requirements on a busy firewall at the risk of dropping idle connections early.

- conservative - extremely conservative settings. This avoids dropping idle connections at the expense of greater memory utilization and slightly increased processor utilization.

The default is normal.

set skip on *interface* Skip *all* PF processing on *interface*. This can be useful on loopback interfaces where filtering, normalization, queueing, etc, are not required. This option can be used multiple times. By default this option is not set. This feature was added in PF 3.7.

set state-policy *option* Sets PF's behavior when it comes to keeping state. This behavior can be overridden on a per rule basis. See the Keeping State section on page 33.

- if-bound - states are bound to the interface they're created on. If traffic matches a state table entry but is not crossing the interface recorded in that state entry, the match is rejected. The packet must then match a filter rule or will be dropped/rejected altogether.

- group-bound - same behavior as if-bound except packets are allowed to cross interfaces in the same group, i.e., all ppp interfaces, etc.

- floating - states can match packets on any interface. As long as the packet matches a state entry and is passing in the same direction as it was on the interface when the state was created, it does not matter what interface it's crossing, it will pass.

The default is floating.

set timeout *option value* Set various timeouts (in seconds).

- interval - seconds between purges of expired states and packet fragments. The default is 10.
- frag - seconds before an unassembled fragment is expired. The default is 30.
- src.track - seconds to keep a source tracking entry in memory after the last state expires. The default is 0 (zero).

9.3. Examples

The following are some examples of using the set command to tune PF:

```
set timeout interval 10
set timeout frag 30
set limit { frags 5000, states 2500 }
set optimization high-latency
set block-policy return
set loginterface dc0
set fingerprints /etc/pf.os.test
set skip on lo0
set state-policy if-bound
```

10. Scrub (Packet Normalization)

10.1. Overview

"Scrubbing" is the normalization of packets so there are no ambiguities in interpretation by the ultimate destination of the packet. The scrub directive also reassembles fragmented packets, protecting some operating systems from some forms of attack, and drops TCP packets that have invalid flag combinations.

10.2. Scrubbing packets

A simple form of the scrub directive:

```
scrub in all
```

This will scrub all incoming packets on all interfaces.

One reason not to scrub on an interface is if one is passing NFS through PF. Some platforms send (and expect) strange packets – fragmented packets with the "do not fragment" bit set, which are (properly) rejected by scrub. This can be resolved by use of the no-df option. Another reason is some multi-player games have connection problems passing through PF with scrub enabled. Other than these somewhat unusual cases, scrubbing all packets is *highly recommended* practice.

The scrub directive syntax is very similar to the filtering syntax which makes it easy to selectively scrub certain packets and not others. The no keyword can be used in front of scrub to specify packets that will not be scrubbed. Just as with nat rules, the first matching rule wins.

More on the principle and concepts of scrubbing can be found in the *Network Intrusion Detection: Evasion, Traffic Normalization, and*

End-to-End Protocol Semantics paper at
http://www.icir.org/vern/papers/norm-usenix-sec-01-html/index.html.

10.3. scrub Options

Scrub has the following options which can be placed at the end of the scrub rule:

no-df Clears the *don't fragment* bit from the IP packet header. Some operating systems are known to generate fragmented packets with the *don't fragment* bit set. This is particularly true with NFS. Scrub will drop such packets unless the no-df option is specified. Because some operating systems generate *don't fragment* packets with a zero IP identification header field, using no-df in conjunction with random-id is recommended.

random-id Replaces the IP identification field of packets with random values to compensate for operating systems that use predictable values. This option only applies to packets[1] that are not fragmented after the optional packet reassembly.

min-ttl *num* Enforces a minimum Time To Live (TTL) in IP packet headers.

max-mss *num* Enforces a maximum Maximum   Segment Size (MSS) in TCP packet headers.

fragment reassemble Buffers incoming packet fragments and reassembles them into a complete packet before passing them to the filter engine. The advantage is that filter rules only have to deal with complete packets and can ignore fragments. The drawback is the increased memory needed to buffer packet fragments. This is the default behavior when no fragment option is specified. This is also the only fragment option that works with NAT.

---

[1] The random-id option only applies to outgoing packets for PF versions before PF 3.7.

fragment crop Causes duplicate fragments to be dropped and any overlaps to be cropped. Unlike `fragment reassemble`, fragments are not buffered but are passed on as soon as they arrive.

fragment drop-ovl Similar to `fragment crop` except that all duplicate or overlapping fragments will be dropped as well as any further corresponding fragments.

reassemble tcp Statefully normalizes TCP connections. When using `scrub reassemble tcp`, a direction (in/out) may not be specified. The following normalizations are performed:

- Neither side of the connection is allowed to reduce their IP TTL. This is done to protect against an attacker sending a packet such that it reaches the firewall, affects the held state information for the connection, and expires before reaching the destination host. The TTL of all packets is raised to the highest value seen for the connection.

- Modulate RFC 1323[2] timestamps in TCP packet headers with a random number. This can prevent an observer from deducing the uptime of the host or from guessing how many hosts are behind a NAT gateway.

10.4. Examples

```
scrub in on fxp0 all fragment reassemble \
    min-ttl 15 max-mss 1400
scrub in on fxp0 all no-df
scrub    on fxp0 all reassemble tcp
```

---

[2]"TCP Extensions for High Performance," http://www.ietf.org/rfc/rfc1323.txt

11. Anchors

11.1. Overview

In addition to the main ruleset, PF can also evaluate sub rulesets. Since sub rulesets can be manipulated on the fly by using pfctl(8), they provide a convenient way of dynamically altering an active ruleset. Whereas a table is used to hold a dynamic list of addresses, a sub ruleset is used to hold a dynamic set of filter, nat, rdr, and binat rules.

Sub rulesets are attached to the main ruleset by using anchors. There are four types of anchor rules:

- `anchor` *name* - evaluates all filter rules in the anchor name

- `binat-anchor` *name* - evaluates all binat rules in the anchor name

- `nat-anchor` *name* - evaluates all nat rules in the anchor name

- `rdr-anchor` *name* - evaluates all rdr rules in the anchor

Anchors can be nested which allows for sub rulesets to be chained together. Anchor rules will be evaluated relative to the anchor in which they are loaded. For example, anchor rules in the main ruleset will create anchor attachment points with the main ruleset as their parent, and anchor rules loaded from files with the `load anchor` directive will create anchor points with that anchor as their parent.

11.2. Anchors

An anchor is a collection of filter and/or translation rules, tables, and other anchors that has been assigned a name. When PF comes across an anchor rule in the main ruleset, it will evaluate the rules contained within the anchor point as it evaluates rules in the main ruleset. Processing will then continue in the main ruleset unless the packet matches a filter rule that uses the quick option or a translation rule within the anchor in which case the match will be considered final and will abort the evaluation of rules in both the anchor and the main rulesets.

For example:

```
ext_if = "fxp0"
block on $ext_if all
pass   out on $ext_if all keep state
anchor goodguys
```

This ruleset sets a default deny policy on fxp0 for both incoming and outgoing traffic. Traffic is then statefully passed out and an anchor rule is created named goodguys. Anchors can be populated with rules by two methods:

- using a load rule

- using pfctl(8)

The load rule causes pfctl to populate the specified anchor by reading rules from a text file. The load rule must be placed after the anchor rule. Example:

```
anchor goodguys
load anchor goodguys from "/etc/anchor-goodguys-ssh"
```

To add rules to an anchor using pfctl, the following type of command can be used:

```
# echo "pass in proto tcp from 192.0.2.3 to any \
  port 22" | pfctl -a goodguys -f -
```

Rules can also be saved and loaded from a text file. For example:

```
# pfctl -a goodguys -f /etc/anchor-goodguys-www
```

Where the example /etc/anchor-goodguys-www file contains:

```
pass in proto tcp from 192.0.2.3 to any port 80
pass in proto tcp from 192.0.2.4 to any port { 80 443 }
```

Filter and translation rules can be loaded into an anchor using the same syntax and options as rules loaded into the main ruleset. One caveat, however, is that any macros that are used must also be defined within the anchor itself; macros that are defined in the parent ruleset are not visible from the anchor.

Since anchors can be nested, it's possible to specify that all child anchors within a specified anchor be evaluated:

```
anchor "spam/*"
```

This syntax causes each rule within each anchor attached to the spam anchor to be evaluated. The child anchors will be evaluated in alphabetical order but are not descended into recursively. Anchors are always evaluated relative to the anchor in which they're defined.

Each anchor, as well as the main ruleset, exist separately from the other rulesets. Operations done on one ruleset, such as flushing the rules, do not affect any of the others. In addition, removing an anchor point from the main ruleset does not destroy the anchor or any child anchors that are attached to that anchor. An anchor is not destroyed until it's flushed of all rules using pfctl(8) and there are no child anchors within the anchor.

11.3. Anchor Options

Optionally, anchor rules can specify interface, protocol, source and destination address, tag, etc., using the same syntax as filter rules. When such information is given, anchor rules are only processed if the packet matches the anchor rule's definition. For example:

```
ext_if = "fxp0"
block on $ext_if all
pass  out on $ext_if all keep state
anchor ssh in on $ext_if proto tcp from any to any \
   port 22
```

The rules in the anchor ssh are only evaluated for TCP packets destined for port 22 that come in on fxp0. Rules are then added to the anchor like so:

```
# echo "pass in from 192.0.2.10 to any" \
| pfctl -a ssh -f -
```

So, even though the filter rule doesn't specify an interface, protocol, or port, the host 192.0.2.10 will only be permitted to connect using SSH because of the anchor rule's definition.

11.4. Manipulating Anchors

Manipulation of anchors is performed via pfctl. It can be used to add and remove rules from an anchor without reloading the main ruleset.
   To list all the rules in the anchor named ssh:

```
# pfctl -a ssh -s rules
```

To flush all filter rules from the same anchor:

```
# pfctl -a ssh -F rules
```

For a full list of commands, read the pfctl(8) manual page.

12. Packet Queueing and Prioritization

12.1. Queueing

To queue something is to store it, in order, while it awaits processing. In a computer network, when data packets are sent out from a host, they enter a queue where they await processing by the operating system. The operating system then decides which queue and which packet(s) from that queue should be processed. The order in which the operating system selects the packets to process can affect network performance. For example, imagine a user running two network applications: SSH and FTP. Ideally, the SSH packets should be processed before the FTP packets because of the time-sensitive nature of SSH; when a key is typed in the SSH client, an immediate response is expected, but an FTP transfer being delayed by a few extra seconds hardly bears any notice.

But what happens if the router handling these connections processes a large chunk of packets from the FTP connection before processing the SSH connection? Packets from the SSH connection will remain in the queue (or possibly be dropped by the router if the queue isn't big enough to hold all of the packets) and the SSH session may appear to lag or slow down. By modifying the queueing strategy being used, network bandwidth can be shared fairly between different applications, users, and computers.

Note that queueing is only useful for packets in the *outbound* direction. Once a packet arrives on an interface in the inbound direction it's already too late to queue it – it has already consumed network bandwidth to get to the interface that just received it. The only solution is to enable queueing on the adjacent router or, if the host that received the packet is acting as a router, to enable queueing on the internal interface where packets exit the router.

12.2. Schedulers

The scheduler is what decides which queues to process and in what order. By default, PF uses a First In First Out (FIFO) scheduler. A FIFO queue works like the line-up at a supermarket's checkout – the first item into the queue is the first processed. As new packets arrive, they are added to the end of the queue. If the queue becomes full, and here the analogy with the supermarket stops, newly arriving packets are dropped. This is known as tail-drop.

PF supports two additional schedulers:[1]

- Class Based Queueing

- Priority Queueing

Class Based Queueing

Class Based Queueing (CBQ) is a queueing algorithm that divides a network connection's bandwidth among multiple queues or classes. Each queue then has traffic assigned to it based on source or destination address, port number, protocol, etc. A queue may optionally be configured to borrow bandwidth from its parent queue if the parent is being under-utilized. Queues are also given a priority such that those containing interactive traffic, such as SSH, can have their packets processed ahead of queues containing bulk traffic, such as FTP.

CBQ queues are arranged in an hierarchical manner. At the top of the hierarchy is the root queue which defines the total amount of bandwidth available. Child queues are created under the root queue, each of which can be assigned some portion of the root queue's bandwidth. For example, queues might be defined as follows:

Root Queue (2Mbps)

      Queue A (1Mbps)

      Queue B (500Kbps)

---

[1]Note that some implementations of PF are not integrated with ALTQ and some do not provide PF-based queueing schedulers by default.

Queue C (500Kbps)

In this case, the total available bandwidth is set to 2 megabits per second (Mbps). This bandwidth is then split among three child queues.

The hierarchy can further be expanded by defining queues within queues. To split bandwidth equally among different users and also classify their traffic so that certain protocols don't starve others for bandwidth, a queueing structure like this might be defined:

Root Queue (2Mbps)
    UserA (1Mbps)
      ssh (50Kbps)
      bulk (950Kbps)
    UserB (1Mbps)
      audio (250Kbps)
      bulk (750Kbps)
        http (100Kbps)
        other (650Kbps)

Note that at each level the sum of the bandwidth assigned to each of the queues is not more than the bandwidth assigned to the parent queue.

A queue can be configured to borrow bandwidth from its parent if the parent has excess bandwidth available due to it not being used by the other child queues. Consider a queueing setup like this:

Root Queue (2Mbps)
    UserA (1Mbps)
      ssh (100Kbps)
      ftp (900Kbps, borrow)
    UserB (1Mbps)

If traffic in the ftp queue exceeds 900Kbps and traffic in the UserA queue is less than 1Mbps (because the ssh queue is using less than its assigned 100Kbps), the ftp queue will borrow the excess bandwidth from UserA. In this way, the ftp queue is able to use more than its assigned bandwidth when it faces overload. When the ssh queue increases its load, the borrowed bandwidth will be returned.

CBQ assigns each queue a priority level. Queues with a higher priority are preferred during congestion over queues with a lower priority as long as both queues share the same parent (in other words, as long as both queues are on the same branch in the hierarchy). Queues with the same priority are processed in a round-robin fashion. For example:

Root Queue (2Mbps)
UserA (1Mbps, priority 1)
ssh (100Kbps, priority 5)
ftp (900Kbps, priority 3)
UserB (1Mbps, priority 1)

CBQ will process the UserA and UserB queues in a round-robin fashion – neither queue will be preferred over the other. During the time when the UserA queue is being processed, CBQ will also process its child queues. In this case, the ssh queue has a higher priority and will be given preferential treatment over the ftp queue if the network is congested. Note how the ssh and ftp queues do not have their priorities compared to the UserA and UserB queues because they are not all on the same branch in the hierarchy.

For a more detailed look at the theory behind CBQ, please see *References on CBQ* at http://www.icir.org/floyd/cbq.html.

Priority Queueing

Priority Queueing (PRIQ) assigns multiple queues to a network interface with each queue being given a unique priority level. A queue with a higher priority is *always* processed ahead of a queue with a lower priority.

The queueing structure in PRIQ is flat – you cannot define queues within queues. The root queue is defined, which sets the total amount of bandwidth that is available, and then sub queues are defined under the root. Consider the following example:

Root Queue (2Mbps)
Queue A (priority 1)
Queue B (priority 2)
Queue C (priority 3)

The root queue is defined as having 2Mbps of bandwidth available to it and three subqueues are defined. The queue with the highest priority (the highest priority number) is served first. Once all the packets in that queue are processed, or if the queue is found to be empty, PRIQ moves onto the queue with the next highest priority. Within a given queue, packets are processed in a First In First Out (FIFO) manner.

It is important to note that when using PRIQ you must plan your queues very carefully. Because PRIQ *always* processes a higher priority queue before a lower priority one, it's possible for a high priority queue to cause packets in a lower priority queue to be delayed or dropped if the high priority queue is receiving a constant stream of packets.

Random Early Detection

Random Early Detection (RED) is a congestion avoidance algorithm. Its job is to avoid network congestion by making sure that the queue doesn't become full. It does this by continually calculating the average length (size) of the queue and comparing it to two thresholds, a minimum threshold and a maximum threshold.

If the average queue size is below the minimum threshold then no packets will be dropped. If the average is above the maximum threshold then *all* newly arriving packets will be dropped. If the average is between the threshold values then packets are dropped based on a probability calculated from the average queue size. In other words, as the average queue size approaches the maximum threshold, more and more packets are dropped. When dropping packets, RED randomly chooses which connections to drop packets from. Connections using larger amounts of bandwidth have a higher probability of having their packets dropped.

RED is useful because it avoids a situation known as global synchronization and it is able to accommodate bursts of traffic. Global synchronization refers to a loss of total throughput due to packets being dropped from several connections at the same time. For example, if congestion occurs at a router carrying traffic for 10 FTP connections and packets from all (or most) of these connections are dropped (as is the case with FIFO queueing), overall throughput will drop sharply. This isn't an ideal situation because it causes all of the FTP connections to reduce their throughput and also means that the network is no longer being used to its maximum potential. RED avoids this by randomly choosing which connections to drop packets from instead of choosing all of them.

Connections using large amounts of bandwidth have a higher chance of their packets being dropped. In this way, high bandwidth connections will be throttled back, congestion will be avoided, and sharp losses of overall throughput will not occur. In addition, RED is able to handle bursts of traffic because it starts to drop packets *before* the queue becomes full. When a burst of traffic comes through there will be enough space in the queue to hold the new packets.

RED should only be used when the transport protocol is capable of responding to congestion indicators from the network. In most cases this means RED should be used to queue TCP traffic and not UDP or ICMP traffic.

For a more detailed look at the theory behind RED, please see *References on RED* at http://www.icir.org/floyd/red.html.

Explicit Congestion Notification

Explicit Congestion Notification (ECN) works in conjunction with RED to notify two hosts communicating over the network of any congestion along the communication path. It does this by enabling RED to set a flag in the packet header instead of dropping the packet. Assuming the sending host has support for ECN, it can then read this flag and throttle back its network traffic accordingly.

For more information on ECN, please refer to RFC 3168, "The Addition of Explicit Congestion Notification (ECN) to IP".[2]

12.3. Configuring Queueing

Since NetBSD 1.6, OpenBSD 3.0, DragonFly 1.2, and FreeBSD 5.3, the Alternate Queueing (ALTQ) framework[3] from the KAME Project has been part of the base system. It provides flexible traffic scheduling and bandwidth rate limiting. Starting with OpenBSD 3.3, ALTQ has been integrated into PF. OpenBSD's ALTQ implementation supports the Class Based Queueing (CBQ) and Priority Queueing (PRIQ)

---

[2]http://www.ietf.org/rfc/rfc3168.txt
[3]See the *ALTQ: Alternate Queueing for BSD UNIX* webpage at http://www.csl.sony.co.jp/person/kjc/kjc/software.html for more information.

schedulers. It also supports Random Early Detection (RED) and Explicit Congestion Notification (ECN).

PF provides the only way to do ALTQ on DragonFly and FreeBSD systems, but a custom kernel is needed. To enable ALTQ and related functionality on DragonFly or FreeBSD, use the following kernel options:[4]

```
options    ALTQ        # ALTQ network traffic shaping
options    ALTQ_CBQ    # Class Based Queueing
options    ALTQ_RED    # Random Early Detection
options    ALTQ_RIO    # RED with IN/OUT bit
options    ALTQ_HFSC   # Hierarchical Fair Service Curve
options    ALTQ_PRIQ   # Priority Queueing
```

Because ALTQ has been merged with PF, PF must be enabled for queueing to work. NetBSD's ALTQ has not yet been integrated with PF. [5] Instructions on how to enable PF can be found in chapter 2.

Queueing is configured in pf.conf. There are two types of directives that are used to configure queueing:

- altq on - enables queueing on an interface, defines which scheduler to use, and creates the root queue

- queue - defines the properties of a child queue

The syntax for the altq on directive is:

```
altq on interface scheduler bandwidth bw \
    qlimit qlim tbrsize size queue { queue_list }
```

- *interface* - the network interface to activate queueing on.

- *scheduler* - the queueing scheduler to use. Possible values are cbq and priq. Only one scheduler may be active on an interface at a time.

---

[4]Note that some of these options are not covered in this book. If using an SMP system, also use the ALTQ_NOPCC option to not use the processor cycle counter. And for debugging support, use the ALTQ_DEBUG option.

[5]Patches and instructions for ALTQ on NetBSD are available via http://nedbsd.nl/~ppostma/pf/altq.html.

- *bw* - the total amount of bandwidth available to the scheduler. This may be specified as an absolute value using the suffixes b, Kb, Mb, and Gb to represent bits, kilobits, megabits, and giga-bits per second, respectively, or as a percentage of the *interface* bandwidth.

- *qlim* - the maximum number of packets to hold in the queue. This parameter is optional. The default is 50.

- *size* - the size of the token bucket regulator in bytes. If not specified, the size is set based on the *interface* bandwidth.

- *queue_list* - a list of child queues to create under the root queue.

For example:

```
altq on fxp0 cbq bandwidth 2Mb queue { std, ssh, ftp }
```

This enables CBQ on the fxp0 interface. The total bandwidth available is set to 2Mbps. Three child queues are defined: std, ssh, and ftp.

The syntax for the queue directive is:

```
queue name [on interface] bandwidth bw \
    [priority pri] [qlimit qlim] \
    scheduler ( sched_options ) { queue_list }
```

- *name* - the name of the queue. This must match the name of one of the queues defined in the altq on directive's *queue_list* . For cbq, it can also match the name of a queue in a previous queue directive's *queue_list*. Queue names must be no longer than 15 characters.

- *interface* - the network interface that the queue is valid on. This value is optional, and when not specified, will make the queue valid on all interfaces.

- *bw* - the total amount of bandwidth available to the queue. This may be specified as an absolute value using the suffixes b, Kb,

Mb, and Gb to represent bits, kilobits, megabits, and gigabits per second, respectively, or as a percentage of the parent queue's bandwidth. This parameter is only applicable when using the cbq scheduler. If not specified, the default is 100% of the parent queue's bandwith.

- *pri* - the priority of the queue. For cbq the priority range is 0 to 7 and for priq the range is 0 to 15. Priority 0 is the lowest priority. When not specified, a default of 1 is used.

- *qlim* - the maximum number of packets to hold in the queue. When not specified, a default of 50 is used.

- *scheduler* - the scheduler being used, either cbq or priq. Must be the same as the root queue.

- *sched_options* - further options may be passed to the scheduler to control its behavior:

    o default - defines a default queue where all packets not matching any other queue will be queued. Exactly one default queue is required.

    o red - enables Random Early Detection (RED) on this queue.

    o rio - enables RED with IN/OUT. In this mode, RED will maintain multiple average queue lengths and multiple threshold values, one for each IP Quality of Service level.

    o ecn - enables Explicit Congestion Notification (ECN) on this queue. Ecn implies red.

    o borrow - the queue can borrow bandwidth from its parent. This can only be specified when using the cbq scheduler.

- *queue_list* - a list of child queues to create under this queue. A *queue_list* may only be defined when using the cbq scheduler.

Continuing with the example above:

```
queue std bandwidth 50% cbq(default)
queue ssh bandwidth 25% { ssh_login, ssh_bulk }
    queue ssh_login bandwidth 25% priority 4 cbq(ecn)
    queue ssh_bulk bandwidth 75% cbq(ecn)
queue ftp bandwidth 500Kb priority 3 cbq(borrow red)
```

Here the parameters of the previously defined child queues are set. The std queue is assigned a bandwidth of 50% of the root queue's bandwidth (or 1Mbps) and is set as the default queue. The ssh queue is assigned 25% of the root queue's bandwidth (500kb) and also contains two child queues: ssh_login and ssh_bulk. The ssh_login queue is given a higher priority than ssh_bulk and both have ECN enabled. The ftp queue is assigned a bandwidth of 500Kbps and given a priority of 3. It can also borrow bandwidth when extra is available and has RED enabled.

Note: Each child queue definition has its bandwidth specified. Without specifying the bandwidth, PF will give the queue 100% of the parent queue's bandwidth. In this situation, that would cause an error when the rules are loaded since if there's a queue with 100% of the bandwidth, no other queue can be defined at that level since there is no free bandwidth to allocate to it.

Assigning Traffic to a Queue

To assign traffic to a queue, the queue keyword is used in conjunction with PF's filter rules. For example, consider a set of filtering rules containing a line such as:

```
pass out on fxp0 from any to any port 22
```

Packets matching that rule can be assigned to a specific queue by using the queue keyword:

```
pass out on fxp0 from any to any port 22 queue ssh
```

When using the queue keyword with block directives, any resulting TCP RST or ICMP Unreachable packets are assigned to the specified queue.

Note that queue designation can happen on an interface other than the one defined in the altq on directive:

```
altq on fxp0 cbq bandwidth 2Mb queue { std, ftp }
queue std bandwidth 500Kb cbq(default)
queue ftp bandwidth 1.5Mb
pass in on dc0 from any to any port 21 queue ftp
```

Queueing is enabled on fxp0 but the designation takes place on dc0. If packets matching the pass rule exit from interface fxp0, they will be queued in the ftp queue. This type of queueing can be very useful on routers.

Normally only one queue name is given with the queue keyword, but if a second name is specified that queue will be used for packets with a Type of Service (ToS) of low-delay and for TCP ACK packets with no data payload. A good example of this is found when using SSH. SSH login sessions will set the ToS to low-delay while SCP and SFTP sessions will not. PF can use this information to queue packets belonging to a login connection in a different queue than non-login connections. This can be useful to prioritize login connection packets over file transfer packets.

```
pass out on fxp0 from any to any port 22 \
   queue(ssh_bulk, ssh_login)
```

This assigns packets belonging to SSH login connections to the ssh_login queue and packets belonging to SCP and SFTP connections to the ssh_bulk queue. SSH login connections will then have their packets processed ahead of SCP and SFTP connections because the ssh_login queue has a higher priority.

Assigning TCP ACK packets to a higher priority queue is useful on asymmetric connections, that is, connections that have different upload and download bandwidths such as ADSL lines. With an ADSL line, if the upload channel is being maxed out and a download is started, the download will suffer because the TCP ACK packets it needs to send will run into congestion when they try to pass through the upload channel. Testing has shown that to achieve the best results, the bandwidth on the upload queue should be set to a value less than what the connection is capable of. For instance, if an ADSL line has a max upload of 640Kbps, setting the root queue's bandwidth to a value such as 600Kb should result in better performance. Trial and error will yield the best bandwidth setting.

When using the queue keyword with rules that keep state such as:

```
pass in on fxp0 proto tcp from any to any port 22 \
    flags S/SA keep state queue ssh
```

PF will record the queue in the state table entry so that packets traveling back out fxp0 that match the stateful connection will end up in the ssh queue. Note that even though the queue keyword is being used on a rule filtering incoming traffic, the goal is to specify a queue for the corresponding outgoing traffic; the above rule does not queue incoming packets.

12.4. Example #1: Small, Home Network

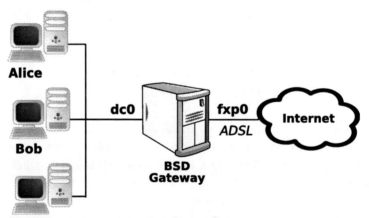

In this example, OpenBSD, NetBSD, FreeBSD or DragonFly is being used on an Internet gateway for a small home network with three workstations. The gateway is performing packet filtering and NAT duties. The Internet connection is via an ADSL line running at 2Mbps down and 640Kbps up.

The queueing policy for this network:

- Reserve 80Kbps of download bandwidth for Bob so he can play his online games without being lagged by Alice or Charlie's downloads. Allow Bob to use more than 80Kbps when it's available.

- Interactive SSH and instant message traffic will have a higher priority than regular traffic.

- DNS queries and replies will have the second highest priority.

- Outgoing TCP ACK packets will have a higher priority than all other outgoing traffic.

Below is the ruleset that meets this network policy. Note that only the pf.conf directives that apply directly to the above policy are present; nat, rdr, options, etc., are not shown.

```
# Enable queueing on the external interface to control
# traffic going to the Internet. Use the priq scheduler
# to control only priorities. Set the bandwidth to
# 610Kbps to get the best performance out of the TCP
# ACK queue.

altq on fxp0 priq bandwidth 610Kb queue { std_out, \
    ssh_im_out, dns_out, tcp_ack_out }

# Define the parameters for the child queues.
# std_out      - The standard queue. Any filter rule
#                below that does not explicitly specify
#                a queue will have its traffic added to
#                this queue.
# ssh_im_out   - Interactive SSH and various instant
#                message traffic.
# dns_out      - DNS queries.
# tcp_ack_out  - TCP ACK packets with no data payload.

queue std_out      priq(default)
queue ssh_im_out   priority 4 priq(red)
queue dns_out      priority 5
queue tcp_ack_out  priority 6
```

```
# Enable queueing on the internal interface to control
# traffic coming in from the Internet. Use the cbq
# scheduler to control bandwidth. Max bandwidth is 2Mbps.

altq on dc0 cbq bandwidth 2Mb \
    queue { std_in, ssh_im_in, dns_in, bob_in }

# Define the parameters for the child queues.
# std_in       - The standard queue. Any filter rule
#                below that does not explicitly specify
#                a queue will have its traffic added
#                to this queue.
# ssh_im_in    - Interactive SSH and various instant
#                message traffic.
# dns_in       - DNS replies.
# bob_in       - Bandwidth reserved for Bob's
#                workstation. Allow him to borrow.

queue std_in    bandwidth 1.6Mb cbq(default)
queue ssh_im_in bandwidth 200Kb priority 4
queue dns_in    bandwidth 120Kb priority 5
queue bob_in    bandwidth 80Kb cbq(borrow)

# ... in the filtering section of pf.conf ...

alice         = "192.168.0.2"
bob           = "192.168.0.3"
charlie       = "192.168.0.4"
local_net     = "192.168.0.0/24"
ssh_ports     = "{ 22 2022 }"
im_ports      = "{ 1863 5190 5222 }"

# Filter rules for fxp0 inbound.
block in on fxp0 all

# Filter rules for fxp0 outbound.
block out on fxp0 all
```

```
pass  out on fxp0 inet proto tcp from (fxp0) to any \
   flags S/SA keep state queue(std_out, tcp_ack_out)
pass  out on fxp0 inet proto { udp icmp } \
   from (fxp0) to any keep state
pass  out on fxp0 inet proto { tcp udp } \
   from (fxp0) to any port domain \
   keep state queue dns_out
pass  out on fxp0 inet proto tcp from (fxp0) \
   to any port $ssh_ports flags S/SA \
   keep state queue(std_out, ssh_im_out)
pass  out on fxp0 inet proto tcp from (fxp0) to any \
   port $im_ports flags S/SA keep state \
   queue(ssh_im_out, tcp_ack_out)

# Filter rules for dc0 inbound.
block in on dc0 all
pass  in on dc0 from $local_net

# Filter rules for dc0 outbound.
block out on dc0 all
pass  out on dc0 from any to $local_net
pass  out on dc0 proto { tcp udp } from any \
   port domain to $local_net queue dns_in
pass  out on dc0 proto tcp from any \
   port $ssh_ports to $local_net \
   queue(std_in, ssh_im_in)
pass  out on dc0 proto tcp from any \
   port $im_ports to $local_net queue ssh_im_in
pass  out on dc0 from any to $bob queue bob_in
```

12.5. Example #2: Company Network

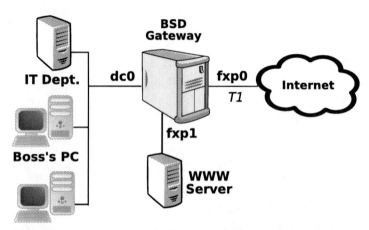

In this example, the BSD host is acting as a firewall for a company network. The company runs a WWW server in the DMZ portion of their network where customers upload their websites via FTP. The IT department has their own subnet connected to the main network, and the boss has a PC on his desk that's used for email and surfing the web. The connection to the Internet is via a T1 line running at 1.5Mbps in both directions. All other network segments are using Fast Ethernet (100Mbps).

The network administrator has decided on the following policy:

- Limit all traffic between the WWW server and the Internet to 500Kbps in each direction.

  - Allot 250Kbps to HTTP traffic.

  - Allot 250Kbps to "other" traffic (i.e., non-HTTP traffic)

  - Allow either queue to borrow up to the full 500Kbps.

  - Give HTTP traffic between the WWW server and the Internet a higher priority than other traffic between the WWW server and the Internet (such as FTP uploads).

- Traffic between the WWW server and the internal network can use up to the full 100Mbps that the network offers.

- Reserve 500Kbps for the IT Dept network so they can download the latest software updates in a timely manner. They should be able to use more than 500Kbps when extra bandwidth is available.

- Give traffic between the boss's PC and the Internet a higher priority than other traffic to/from the Internet.

Below is the ruleset that meets this network policy. Note that only the pf.conf directives that apply directly to the above policy are present; nat, rdr, options, etc., are not shown.

```
# Enable queueing on the external interface to queue
# packets going out to the Internet. Use the cbq
# scheduler so that the bandwidth use of each queue
# can be controlled. The max outgoing bandwidth is
# 1.5Mbps.

altq on fxp0 cbq bandwidth 1.5Mb \
    queue { std_ext, www_ext, boss_ext }

# Define the parameters for the child queues.
# std_ext        - The standard queue. Also the default
#                  queue for outgoing traffic on fxp0.
# www_ext        - Container queue for WWW server
#                  queues. Limit to 500Kbps.
#   www_ext_http - HTTP traffic from the WWW server;
#                  higher priority.
#   www_ext_misc - All non-HTTP traffic from the WWW
#                  server.
# boss_ext       - Traffic coming from the boss's
#                  computer.

queue std_ext bandwidth 500Kb cbq(default borrow)
queue www_ext bandwidth 500Kb \
    { www_ext_http, www_ext_misc }
  queue www_ext_http bandwidth 50% priority 3 \
    cbq(red borrow)
```

93

```
   queue www_ext_misc bandwidth 50% priority 1 \
       cbq(borrow)
queue boss_ext bandwidth 500Kb priority 3 \
       cbq(borrow)


# Enable queueing on the internal interface to control
# traffic coming from the Internet or the DMZ. Use the
# cbq scheduler to control the bandwidth of each queue.
# Bandwidth on this interface is set to the maximum.
# Traffic coming from the DMZ will be able to use all
# of this bandwidth while traffic coming from the
# Internet will be limited to 1.0Mbps (because 0.5Mbps
# (500Kbps) is being allocated to fxp1).

altq on dc0 cbq bandwidth 100% \
   queue { net_int, www_int }


# Define the parameters for the child queues.
# net_int    - Container queue for traffic from
#                the Internet. Bandwidth is 1.0Mbps.
#    std_int - The standard queue. Also the default
#                queue for outgoing traffic on dc0.
#    it_int  - Traffic to the IT Dept network; reserve
#                500Kbps for them.
#    boss_int - Traffic to the boss's PC; assign a
#                higher priority.
# www_int    - Traffic from the WWW server in the DMZ;
#                full speed.

queue net_int    bandwidth 1.0Mb \
       { std_int, it_int, boss_int }
  queue std_int  bandwidth 250Kb cbq(default borrow)
  queue it_int   bandwidth 500Kb cbq(borrow)
  queue boss_int bandwidth 250Kb priority 3 cbq(borrow)
queue www_int    bandwidth 99Mb cbq(red borrow)


# Enable queueing on the DMZ interface to control
```

```
# traffic destined for the WWW server. CBQ will be
# used on this interface since detailed control of
# bandwidth is necessary. Bandwidth on this interface
# is set to the maximum. Traffic from the internal
# network will be able to use all of this bandwidth
# while traffic from the Internet will be limited
# to 500Kbps.

altq on fxp1 cbq bandwidth 100% \
   queue { internal_dmz, net_dmz }

# Define the parameters for the child queues.
# internal_dmz   - Traffic from the internal network.
# net_dmz        - Container queue for traffic from
#                  the Internet.
#   net_dmz_http - HTTP traffic; higher priority.
#   net_dmz_misc - All non-HTTP traffic. This is also
#                  the default queue.

queue internal_dmz    bandwidth 99Mb cbq(borrow)
queue net_dmz         bandwidth 500Kb \
      { net_dmz_http, net_dmz_misc }
  queue net_dmz_http bandwidth 50% priority 3 \
      cbq(red borrow)
  queue net_dmz_misc bandwidth 50% priority 1 \
      cbq(default borrow)


# ... in the filtering section of pf.conf ...

main_net  = "192.168.0.0/24"
it_net    = "192.168.1.0/24"
int_nets  = "{ 192.168.0.0/24, 192.168.1.0/24 }"
dmz_net   = "10.0.0.0/24"

boss      = "192.168.0.200"
wwwserv   = "10.0.0.100"
```

```
# Default deny.
block on { fxp0, fxp1, dc0 } all

# Filter rules for fxp0 inbound.
pass in on fxp0 proto tcp from any to $wwwserv \
   port { 21, > 49151 } flags S/SA keep state \
   queue www_ext_misc
pass in on fxp0 proto tcp from any to $wwwserv port 80 \
   flags S/SA keep state queue www_ext_http

# Filter rules for fxp0 outbound.
pass out on fxp0 from $int_nets to any keep state
pass out on fxp0 from $boss to any keep state \
   queue boss_ext

# Filter rules for dc0 inbound.
pass in on dc0 from $int_nets to any keep state
pass in on dc0 from $it_net to any queue it_int
pass in on dc0 from $boss to any queue boss_int
pass in on dc0 proto tcp from $int_nets to $wwwserv \
   port { 21, 80, > 49151 } flags S/SA keep state \
   queue www_int

# Filter rules for dc0 outbound.
pass out on dc0 from dc0 to $int_nets

# Filter rules for fxp1 inbound.
pass in on fxp1 proto { tcp, udp } from $wwwserv \
   to any port 53 keep state

# Filter rules for fxp1 outbound.
pass out on fxp1 proto tcp from any to $wwwserv \
   port { 21, > 49151 } flags S/SA keep state \
   queue net_dmz_misc
pass out on fxp1 proto tcp from any to $wwwserv \
   port 80 flags S/SA keep state queue net_dmz_http
```

```
pass out on fxp1 proto tcp from $int_nets to $wwwserv \
    port { 80, 21, > 49151 } flags S/SA keep state \
    queue internal_dmz
```

13. Address Pools and Load Balancing

13.1. Overview

An address pool is a supply of two or more addresses whose use is shared among a group of users. An address pool can be specified as the redirection address in `rdr` rules, as the translation address in `nat` rules, and as the target address in `route-to`, `reply-to`, and `dup-to` filter options.

There are four methods for using an address pool:

- `bitmask` - grafts the network portion of the pool address over top of the address that is being modified (source address for nat rules, destination address for rdr rules). Example: if the address pool is 192.0.2.1/24 and the address being modified is 10.0.0.50, then the resulting address will be 192.0.2.50. If the address pool is 192.0.2.1/25 and the address being modified is 10.0.0.130, then the resulting address will be 192.0.2.2.

- `random` - randomly selects an address from the pool.

- `source-hash` - uses a hash of the source address to determine which address to use from the pool. This method ensures that a given source address is always mapped to the same pool address. The key that is fed to the hashing algorithm can optionally be specified after the source-hash keyword in hex format or as a string. By default, pfctl(8) will generate a random key every time the ruleset is loaded.

- `round-robin` - loops through the address pool in sequence. This is the default method and also the only method allowed when the address pool is specified using a table.

Except for the round-robin method, the address pool must be expressed as a CIDR (Classless Inter-Domain Routing) network block. The round-robin method will accept multiple individual addresses using a list or table.

The sticky-address option can be used with the random and round-robin pool types to ensure that a particular source address is always mapped to the same redirection address.

13.2. NAT Address Pool

An address pool can be used as the translation address in nat rules. Connections will have their source address translated to an address from the pool based on the chosen method. This can be useful in situations where PF is performing NAT for a very large network. Since the number of NATed connections per translation address is limited, adding additional translation addresses will allow the NAT gateway to scale to serve a larger number of users.

In this example, a pool of two addresses is being used to translate outgoing packets. For each outgoing connection, PF will rotate through the addresses in a round-robin manner.

```
nat on $ext_if inet from any \
   to any -> { 192.0.2.5, 192.0.2.10 }
```

One drawback with this method is that successive connections from the same internal address will not always be translated to the same translation address. This can cause interference, for example, when browsing websites that track user logins based on IP address. An alternate approach is to use the source-hash method so that each internal address is always translated to the same translation address. To do this, the address pool must be a CIDR network block.

```
nat on $ext_if inet from any \
   to any -> 192.0.2.4/31 source-hash
```

This nat rule uses the address pool 192.0.2.4/31 (192.0.2.4 - 192.0.2.5) as the translation address for outgoing packets. Each internal address will always be translated to the same translation address because of the source-hash keyword.

13.3. Load Balance Incoming Connections

Address pools can also be used to load balance incoming connections. For example, incoming web server connections can be distributed across a web server farm:

```
web_servers = "{ 10.0.0.10, 10.0.0.11, 10.0.0.13 }"
rdr on $ext_if proto tcp from any to any \
  port 80 -> $web_servers round-robin sticky-address
```

Successive connections will be redirected to the web servers in a round-robin manner with connections from the same source being sent to the same web server. This "sticky connection" will exist as long as there are states that refer to this connection. Once the states expire, so will the sticky connection. Further connections from that host will be redirected to the next web server in the round robin.

13.4. Load Balance Outgoing Traffic

Address pools can be used in combination with the route-to filter option to load balance two or more Internet connections when a proper multi-path routing protocol (like BGP4) is unavailable. By using route-to with a round-robin address pool, outbound connections can be evenly distributed among multiple outbound paths.

One additional piece of information that's needed to do this is the IP address of the adjacent router on each Internet connection. This is fed to the route-to option to control the destination of outgoing packets.

The following example balances outgoing traffic across two Internet connections:

```
lan_net = "192.168.0.0/24"
int_if  = "dc0"
ext_if1 = "fxp0"
ext_if2 = "fxp1"
ext_gw1 = "68.146.224.1"
ext_gw2 = "142.59.76.1"
pass in on $int_if route-to \
```

```
{ ($ext_if1 $ext_gw1), ($ext_if2 $ext_gw2) } \
round-robin from $lan_net to any keep state
```

The `route-to` option is used on traffic coming *in* on the *internal* interface to specify the outgoing network interfaces that traffic will be balanced across along with their respective gateways. Note that the `route-to` option must be present on *each* filter rule that traffic is to be balanced for. Return packets will be routed back to the same external interface that they exited (this is done by the ISPs) and will be routed back to the internal network normally.

To ensure that packets with a source address belonging to $ext_if1 are always routed to $ext_gw1 (and similarly for $ext_if2 and $ext_gw2), the following two lines should be included in the ruleset:

```
pass out on $ext_if1 route-to ($ext_if2 $ext_gw2) \
   from $ext_if2 to any
pass out on $ext_if2 route-to ($ext_if1 $ext_gw1) \
   from $ext_if1 to any
```

Finally, NAT can also be used on each outgoing interface:

```
nat on $ext_if1 from $lan_net to any -> ($ext_if1)
nat on $ext_if2 from $lan_net to any -> ($ext_if2)
```

A complete example that load balances outgoing traffic might look something like this:

```
lan_net = "192.168.0.0/24"
int_if  = "dc0"
ext_if1 = "fxp0"
ext_if2 = "fxp1"
ext_gw1 = "68.146.224.1"
ext_gw2 = "142.59.76.1"


#  Nat outgoing connections on each internet interface.
nat on $ext_if1 from $lan_net to any -> ($ext_if1)
nat on $ext_if2 from $lan_net to any -> ($ext_if2)
```

```
#  Default deny.
block in  from any to any
block out from any to any

#  Pass all outgoing packets on internal interface.
pass out on $int_if from any to $lan_net

#  Pass in quick any packets destined for the gateway
#  itself.
pass in quick on $int_if from $lan_net to $int_if
#  Load balance outgoing tcp traffic from internal
#  network.
pass in on $int_if route-to \
    { ($ext_if1 $ext_gw1), ($ext_if2 $ext_gw2) } \
    round-robin proto tcp from $lan_net to any \
    flags S/SA modulate state

#  Load balance outgoing udp and icmp traffic from
#  internal network.
pass in on $int_if route-to \
    { ($ext_if1 $ext_gw1), ($ext_if2 $ext_gw2) } \
    round-robin proto { udp, icmp } from $lan_net \
    to any keep state

#  General "pass out" rules for external interfaces.
pass out on $ext_if1 proto tcp from any to any \
    flags S/SA modulate state
pass out on $ext_if1 proto { udp, icmp } from any \
    to any keep state
pass out on $ext_if2 proto tcp from any to any \
    flags S/SA modulate state
pass out on $ext_if2 proto { udp, icmp } from any \
    to any keep state

#  Route packets from any IPs on $ext_if1 to $ext_gw1
#  and the same for $ext_if2 and $ext_gw2.
pass out on $ext_if1 route-to ($ext_if2 $ext_gw2) \
```

```
    from $ext_if2 to any
pass out on $ext_if2 route-to ($ext_if1 $ext_gw1) \
    from $ext_if1 to any
```

14. Packet Tagging (Policy Filtering)

14.1. Overview

Packet tagging is a way of marking packets with an internal identifier that can later be used in filter and translation rule criteria. With tagging, it's possible to do such things as create "trusts" between interfaces and determine if packets have been processed by translation rules. It's also possible to move away from rule-based filtering and to start doing policy-based filtering.

14.2. Assigning Tags to Packets

To add a tag to a packet, use the tag keyword:

```
pass in on $int_if all tag INTERNAL_NET keep state
```

The tag INTERNAL_NET will be added to any packet which matches the above rule.

A tag can also be assigned using a macro. For instance:

```
name = "INTERNAL_NET"
 pass in on $int_if all tag $name keep state
```

There are a set of predefined macros which can also be used.

- $if - The interface

- $srcaddr - Source IP address

- $dstaddr - Destination IP address

- $srcport - The source port specification

- $dstport - The destination port specification

- $proto - The protocol

- $nr - The rule number

These macros are expanded at ruleset load time and not at runtime. Tagging follows these rules:

- Tags are "sticky". Once a tag is applied to a packet by a matching rule it is never removed. It can, however, be replaced with a different tag.

- Because of a tag's "stickiness", a packet can have a tag even if the last matching rule doesn't use the tag keyword.

- A packet is only ever assigned a maximum of one tag at a time.

- Tags are *internal* identifiers. Tags are not sent out over the wire.

Take the following ruleset as an example.

```
(1) pass in on $int_if tag INT_NET keep state
(2) pass in quick on $int_if proto tcp to port 80 tag \
        INT_NET_HTTP keep state
(3) pass in quick on $int_if from 192.168.1.5 \
        keep state
```

- Packets coming in on $int_if will be assigned a tag of INT_NET by rule #1.

- TCP packets coming in on $int_if and destined for port 80 will first be assigned a tag of INT_NET by rule #1. That tag will then be replaced with the INT_NET_HTTP tag by rule #2.

- Packets coming in on $int_if from 192.168.1.5 will be passed by rule #3 since it's the last matching rule. However, those packets will be tagged with the INT_NET_HTTP tag if they were destined for TCP port 80, otherwise they'll be tagged with the INT_NET tag.

In addition to applying tags with filter rules, the nat, rdr, and binat translation rules can also apply tags to packets by using the tag keyword.

14.3. Checking for Applied Tags

To check for previously applied tags, use the `tagged` keyword:

```
pass out on $ext_if tagged INT_NET keep state
```

Outgoing packets on $ext_if must be tagged with the INT_NET tag in order to match the above rule. Inverse matching can also be done by using the ! operator:

```
pass out on $ext_if ! tagged WIFI_NET keep state
```

Translation rules (nat/rdr/binat) can also use the tagged keyword to match packets.

14.4. Policy Filtering

Policy filtering takes a different approach to writing a filter ruleset. A policy is defined which sets the rules for what types of traffic is passed and what types are blocked. Packets are then classified into the policy based on the traditional criteria of source/destination IP address/port, protocol, etc. For example, examine the following firewall policy:

- Traffic from the internal LAN to the Internet is permitted (LAN_INET) and must be translated (LAN_INET_NAT).

- Traffic from the internal LAN to the DMZ is permitted (LAN_DMZ).

- Traffic from the Internet to servers in the DMZ is permitted (INET_DMZ).

- Traffic from the Internet that's being redirected to spamd(8) is permitted (SPAMD).[1]

---

[1] This is OpenBSD's spam deferral daemon, not the SpamAssassin daemon. See chapter 19 for more information.

- All other traffic is blocked

Note how the policy covers *all* traffic that will be passing through the firewall. The item in parentheses indicates the tag that will be used for that policy item.

Filter and translation rules now need to be written to classify packets into the policy.

```
rdr on $ext_if proto tcp from <spamd> to port smtp \
   tag SPAMD -> 127.0.0.1 port 8025
nat on $ext_if tag LAN_INET_NAT \
   tagged LAN_INET -> ($ext_if)
block all
pass in on $int_if from $int_net tag LAN_INET \
   keep state
pass in on $int_if from $int_net to $dmz_net \
   tag LAN_DMZ keep state
pass in on $ext_if proto tcp to $www_server \
   port 80 tag INET_DMZ keep state
```

Now the rules that define the policy are set.

```
pass in  quick on $ext_if tagged SPAMD keep state
pass out quick on $ext_if tagged LAN_INET_NAT \
   keep state
pass out quick on $dmz_if tagged LAN_DMZ keep state
pass out quick on $dmz_if tagged INET_DMZ keep state
```

Now that the whole ruleset is setup, changes are a matter of modifying the classification rules. For example, if a POP3/SMTP server is added to the DMZ, it will be necessary to add classification rules for POP3 and SMTP traffic, like so:

```
mail_server = "192.168.0.10"
   ...
pass in on $ext_if proto tcp to $mail_server \
   port { smtp, pop3 } tag INET_DMZ keep state
```

Email traffic will now be passed as part of the INET_DMZ policy entry.

The complete ruleset:

```
# Macros
int_if  = "dc0"
dmz_if  = "dc1"
ext_if  = "ep0"
int_net = "10.0.0.0/24"
dmz_net = "192.168.0.0/24"
www_server = "192.168.0.5"
mail_server = "192.168.0.10"

table <spamd> persist file "/etc/spammers"

# classification -- Classify packets based on the
# defined firewall policy.
rdr on $ext_if proto tcp from <spamd> to port smtp \
    tag SPAMD -> 127.0.0.1 port 8025
nat on $ext_if tag LAN_INET_NAT \
   tagged LAN_INET -> ($ext_if)

block all
pass in on $int_if from $int_net tag LAN_INET \
   keep state
pass in on $int_if from $int_net to $dmz_net \
   tag LAN_DMZ keep state
pass in on $ext_if proto tcp to $www_server \
   port 80 tag INET_DMZ keep state
pass in on $ext_if proto tcp to $mail_server \
   port { smtp, pop3 } tag INET_DMZ keep state

# Policy enforcement -- pass/block based on the
# defined firewall policy.
pass in  quick on $ext_if tagged SPAMD keep state
pass out quick on $ext_if tagged LAN_INET_NAT \
   keep state
```

```
pass out quick on $dmz_if tagged LAN_DMZ keep state
pass out quick on $dmz_if tagged INET_DMZ keep state
```

14.5. Tagging Ethernet Frames

Tagging can be performed at the Ethernet level if the machine doing the tagging and filtering is also acting as a bridge(4). By creating bridge(4) filter rules that use the `tag` keyword, PF can be made to filter based on the source or destination MAC address.

On OpenBSD, bridge(4) rules are created using the brconfig(8) command, for example:

```
# brconfig bridge0 rule pass in on fxp0 \
    src 0:de:ad:be:ef:0 tag USER1
```

And then in pf.conf:

```
pass in on fxp0 tagged USER1
```

Note that on NetBSD, PF in bridging mode is supported, but you need to compile a new kernel to enable packet filtering on a bridge. See page 7 for more information. After configuring the bridge, on NetBSD, use the brconfig(8) command to enable packet filtering on the bridge. On NetBSD, the brconfig(8) "ipf" argument enables packet filtering with pfil(9)[2] on the bridge. It passes all ARP and RARP packets through the bridge while filtering IP and ICMP packets.

```
# brconfig bridge0 ipf
```

Now PF should be able to filter packets on the interfaces configured as the bridge. Note that it's only needed to filter on one interface because the same data goes through both interfaces.

---

[2]pfil(9) is a packet filter framework that allows packets to be processed.

15. Logging

15.1. Overview

Packet logging in PF is done by pflogd(8) which listens on the pflog0 interface and writes packets to a log file (normally /var/log/pflog) in tcpdump binary format. Filter rules that specify the `log` keyword are logged in this manner.

15.2. Logging Packets

In order to log packets passing through PF, the `log` keyword must be used within NAT/rdr and filter rules. Note that PF can only log packets that it's blocking or passing; you cannot specify a rule that only logs packets.

The `log` keyword causes all packets that match the rule to be logged. In the case where the rule is creating state, only the first packet seen (the one that causes the state to be created) will be logged.

The options that can be given to the log keyword are:

all Causes all matching packets, not just the initial packet, to be logged. Useful for rules that create state.

user Causes the UNIX user-id and group-id that owns the socket that the packet is sourced from or destined to (whichever socket is local) to be logged along with the standard log information.

Options are given in parentheses after the `log` keyword; multiple options can be separated by a comma or space. The `log (all)` feature was added for nat/rdr/binat pass rules in PF 3.8. The same feature was already available for filter rules in older versions of PF, but it is called "`log-all`" instead. Also, `log (user)` is also new for PF 3.8.

```
pass in log (all) on $ext_if inet proto tcp \
   to $ext_if port 22 keep state
```

This example above logs all incoming packets destined to port 22.

15.3. Reading a Log File

The log file written by pflogd is in binary format and cannot be read using a text editor. Tcpdump (or Ethereal) can be used to view the log.

To view the log file:

```
# tcpdump -n -e -ttt -r /var/log/pflog
```

Note that using tcpdump to watch the pflog file does *not* give a real-time display. A real-time display of logged packets is achieved by using the pflog0 interface:

```
# tcpdump -n -e -ttt -i pflog0
```

Note: When examining the logs, special care should be taken with tcpdump's verbose protocol decoding (activated via the -v command line option). Tcpdump's protocol decoders do not have a perfect security history. At least in theory, a delayed attack could be possible via the partial packet payloads recorded by the logging device. It is recommended practice to move the log files off of the firewall machine before examining them in this way.

Additional care should also be taken to secure access to the logs. By default, pflogd will record 96 bytes of the packet in the log file. Access to the logs could provide partial access to sensitive packet payloads (like telnet or FTP usernames and passwords).

15.4. Filtering Log Output

Because pflogd logs in tcpdump binary format, the full range of tcp-dump features can be used when reviewing the logs. For example, to only see packets that match a certain port:

```
# tcpdump -n -e -ttt -r /var/log/pflog port 80
```

This can be further refined by limiting the display of packets to a certain host and port combination:

```
# tcpdump -n -e -ttt -r /var/log/pflog port 80 and \
    host 192.168.1.3
```

The same idea can be applied when reading from the pflog0 interface:

```
# tcpdump -n -e -ttt -i pflog0 host 192.168.4.2
```

Note that this has no impact on which packets are logged to the pflogd log file; the above commands only display packets as they are being logged.

In addition to using the standard tcpdump filter rules, the tcpdump filter language has been extended for reading pflogd output:

- `ip` - address family is IPv4.

- `ip6` - address family is IPv6.

- `on int` - packet passed through the interface *int*.

- `ifname int` - same as on *int*.

- `ruleset name` - the ruleset/anchor that the packet was matched in.

- `rulenum num` - the filter rule that the packet matched was rule number *num*.

- `action act` - the action taken on the packet. Possible actions are `pass` and `block`.

- `reason res` - the reason that action was taken. Possible reasons are `match`, `bad-offset`, `fragment`, `short`, `normalize`, `memory`, `bad-timestamp`, `congestion`, `ip-option`, `protocksum`, `state-mismatch`, `state-insert`, `state-limit`, `srclimit`, and `synproxy`.[1]

---

[1] PF 3.6 only has `match`, `bad-offset`, `fragment`, `short`, `normalize`, `memory`, and `bad-timestamp`. And PF 3.5 didn't include `bad-timestamp`. For more information, see RFC 1323, "TCP Extensions for High Performance".

- inbound - packet was inbound.

- outbound - packet was outbound.

Example:

```
# tcpdump -n -e -ttt -i pflog0 inbound and \
    action block and on wi0
```

This displays the log, in real-time, of inbound packets that were blocked on the wi0 interface.

15.5. Packet Logging Through Syslog

In many situations, it is desirable to have the firewall logs available in plain text format and/or to send them to a remote logging server. All this can be accomplished with a small shell script, some minor system configuration changes, and syslogd(8), the logging daemon. Syslogd logs in plain text and is also able to log to a remote logging server.

Create the following script:

/etc/pflogrotate

```
#!/bin/sh
PFLOG=/var/log/pflog
FILE=/var/log/pflog5min.$(date "+%Y%m%d%H%M")
# Tell pflogd to flush current log entries to disk.
kill -ALRM $(cat /var/run/pflogd.pid)
if [ -r $PFLOG ] && \
    [ $(stat -f %z $PFLOG) -gt 24 ]; then
    mv $PFLOG $FILE
    # Tell pflogd to close and re-open the log file.
    kill -HUP $(cat /var/run/pflogd.pid)
    tcpdump -n -e -ttt -r $FILE | \
        logger -t pf -p local0.info
    rm $FILE
fi
```

Edit root's cron job:

```
# crontab -u root -e
```

Add the following two lines:

```
# Rotate PF log file every 5 minutes.
0-59/5 * * * * /bin/sh /etc/pflogrotate
```

Add the following line to /etc/syslog.conf:

```
local0.info     /var/log/pflog.txt
```

If you also want to log to a remote log server, add the line:

```
local0.info     @syslogger
```

And make sure host *syslogger* has been defined in the hosts(5) file.

Create the file /var/log/pflog.txt to allow syslog to log to that file, and give it the same permissions as the pflog file.

```
# touch /var/log/pflog.txt
# chmod 600 /var/log/pflog.txt
```

Make syslogd notice the changes by restarting it:

```
# kill -HUP $(cat /var/run/syslog.pid)
```

All logged packets are now sent in plain text to /var/log/pflog.txt. If the second line is added they are sent to the remote logging host *syslogger* as well. The logging is not immediate but it can take up to about five to six minutes (the cron job interval) before the logged packets appear in the file.

The /etc/pflogrotate script now processes and then deletes /var/log/pflog so rotation of pflog by newsyslog(8) is no longer necessary and should be disabled. However, /var/log/pflog.txt replaces /var/log/pflog and rotation of it should be activated. Change /etc/newsyslog.conf to comment out the existing /var/log/pflog rotation entry and to add a new line:

```
/var/log/pflog.txt     600     7     *     24
```

16. Performance

"How much bandwidth can PF handle?"

"How much computer do I need to handle my Internet connection?"

There are no easy answers to those questions. For some applications, a 486/66 with a pair of good ISA NICs could filter and NAT close to 5Mbps, but for other applications a much faster machine with much more efficient PCI NICs might end up being insufficient. The real question is not the number of bits per second but rather the number of packets per second and the complexity of the ruleset.

PF performance is determined by several variables:

Number of packets per second

Almost the same amount of processing needs to be done on a packet with 1500 byte payload as for a packet with a one byte payload. The number of packets per second determines the number of times the state table and, in case of no match there, filter rules have to be evaluated every second, determining the effective demand on the system.

Performance of your system bus

The ISA bus has a maximum bandwidth of 8MB/sec, and when the processor is accessing it, it has to slow itself to the effective speed of a 80286 running at 8MHz, no matter how fast the processor really is. The PCI bus has a much greater effective bandwidth, and has less impact on the processor.

Efficiency of your network card

Some network adapters are just more efficient than others. Realtek 8139 (rl(4)) based cards tend to be relatively poor performers while

Intel 21143 (dc(4)) based cards tend to perform very well. For maximum performance, consider using gigabit Ethernet cards, even if not connecting to gigabit networks, as they have much more advanced buffering.

Complexity and design of your ruleset

The more complex your ruleset, the slower it is. The more packets that are filtered by keep state and quick rules, the better the performance. The more lines that have to be evaluated for each packet, the lower the performance.

CPU and RAM

Barely worth mentioning. As PF is a kernel-based process, it will not use swap space. So, if you have enough RAM, it runs, if not, it panics due to pool(9) exhaustion. Huge amounts of RAM are not needed – 32MB should be plenty for close to 30,000 states, which is a lot of states for a small office or home application. Most users will find a "recycled" computer more than enough for a PF system – a 300MHz system will move a very large number of packets rapidly, at least if backed up with good NICs and a good ruleset.

Benchmarks

People often ask for PF benchmarks. The only benchmark that counts is *your* system performance in *your* environment. A benchmark that doesn't replicate your environment will not properly help you plan your firewall system. The best course of action is to benchmark PF for yourself under the same, or as close as possible to, network conditions that the actual firewall would experience running on the same hardware the firewall would use.

PF is used in some very large, high-traffic applications, and the developers are "power users" of PF. Odds are, it will do very well for you.

17. Issues with FTP

17.1. FTP Modes

FTP is a protocol that dates back to when the Internet was a small, friendly collection of computers and everyone knew everyone else. At that time the need for filtering or tight security wasn't necessary. FTP wasn't designed for filtering, for passing through firewalls, or for working with NAT.

You can use FTP in one of two ways: passive or active. Generally, the choice of active or passive is made to determine who has the problem with firewalling. Realistically, you will have to support both to have happy users.

With active FTP, when a user connects to a remote FTP server and requests information or a file, the FTP server makes a new connection back to the client to transfer the requested data. This is called the *data connection* . To start, the FTP client chooses a random port to receive the data connection on. The client sends the port number it chose to the FTP server and then listens for an incoming connection on that port. The FTP server then initiates a connection to the client's address at the chosen port and transfers the data. This is a problem for users attempting to gain access to FTP servers from behind a NAT gateway. Because of how NAT works, the FTP server initiates the data connection by connecting to the external address of the NAT gateway on the chosen port. The NAT machine will receive this, but because it has no mapping for the packet in its state table, it will drop the packet and won't deliver it to the client.

With passive mode FTP (the default mode with the ftp(1) client), the client requests that the server pick a random port to listen on for the data connection. The server informs the client of the port it has chosen, and the client connects to this port to transfer the data. Unfortunately, this is not always possible or desirable because of the possibility of a firewall in front of the FTP server blocking the incoming data connection. The ftp(1) client uses passive mode by default; to force active mode FTP, use the -A flag with ftp, or set passive mode to "off" by issuing the command "passive off" at the "ftp>" prompt.

More information on filtering FTP and how FTP works in general can be found in the *FTP Reviewed* whitepaper at http://www.pintday.org/whitepapers/ftp-review.shtml.

17.2. FTP Client Behind the Firewall

As indicated earlier, FTP does not go through NAT and firewalls very well.

Packet Filter provides a solution for this situation by redirecting FTP traffic through an FTP proxy server. This process acts to "guide" your FTP traffic through the NAT gateway/firewall, by actively adding needed rules to PF system and removing them when done, by means of the PF anchors. The FTP proxy used by PF is ftp-proxy(8).[1]To activate it, put something like this in the NAT section of pf.conf:

```
nat-anchor "ftp-proxy/*"
rdr-anchor "ftp-proxy/*"
rdr on $int_if proto tcp from any to any \
   port 21 -> 127.0.0.1 port 8021
```

The first two lines are a couple anchors which are used to by ftp-proxy to add rules on-the-fly as needed to manage your FTP traffic. The last line redirects FTP from your clients to the ftp-proxy(8) program, which is listening on your machine to port 8021.

You also need an anchor[2] in the rules section:

```
anchor "ftp-proxy/*"
```

Hopefully it is apparent the proxy server has to be started and running on the BSD box.

On OpenBSD, this is done by inserting the following line in /etc/rc.conf or /etc/rc.conf.local:

---

[1]Earlier versions of OpenBSD used a different proxy of the same name.
[2]Information about anchors is in chapter 11.

```
ftpproxy_flags=""
```

The ftp-proxy program can be started as root to activate it without a reboot.

ftp-proxy listens on port 8021, the same port the above `rdr` statement is sending FTP traffic to. To enable active mode connections, you need the '-r' switch on ftp-proxy(8) (for this you had to run the old proxy with "-u root").

Please note that ftp-proxy(8) is to help FTP clients behind a PF filter; it is not used to handle an FTP server behind a PF filter.

17.2.1. Older ftp-proxy

The previous ftp-proxy doesn't use anchors and is ran via inetd. Be sure to consult your manual page to verify and for further details. To activate it, put something like this in the NAT section of pf.conf:

```
rdr on $int_if proto tcp from any to any \
   port 21 -> 127.0.0.1 port 8021
```

And also enable the service via inetd. If using NetBSD or OpenBSD, this is done by inserting the following line in /etc/inetd.conf:

```
127.0.0.1:8021 stream tcp nowait root \
   /usr/libexec/ftp-proxy ftp-proxy -n
```

On FreeBSD or DragonFly, use the following in /etc/inetd.conf:

```
ftp-proxy stream tcp nowait root \
   /usr/libexec/ftp-proxy ftp-proxy -n
```

With the "ftp-proxy" service defined in /etc/services as tcp port 8021.

Note that the −n switch is only necessary if the BSD machine is performing NAT. Then send a 'HUP' signal to inetd(8) to have it reread its configuration file. One way to send the 'HUP' signal is with the command:

```
kill -HUP `cat /var/run/inetd.pid`
```

17.3. PF "Self-Protecting" an FTP Server

In this case, PF is running on the FTP server itself rather than a dedicated firewall computer. When servicing a passive FTP connection, FTP will use a randomly chosen, high TCP port for incoming data. By default, the native FTP server ftpd(8) uses the range 49152 to 65535. Obviously, these must be passed through the filter rules, along with port 21 (the FTP control port):

```
pass in on $ext_if proto tcp from any to any \
    port 21 keep state
pass in on $ext_if proto tcp from any to any \
    port > 49151 keep state
```

Note that if you desire, you can tighten up that range of ports considerably. In the case of the OpenBSD ftpd(8) program, that is done using the sysctl(8) variables `net.inet.ip.porthifirst` and `net.inet.ip.porthilast`. And on FreeBSD and DragonFly (with their native ftpd servers), this is can be changed with `net.inet.ip.portrange.hifirst` and `net.inet.ip.portrange.hilast`. And NetBSD uses `net.inet.ip.anonportmin` and `net.inet.ip.anonportmax`. (Or for tnftpd/lukemftpd, see the ftpd.conf(5) manual page for "portrange".)

17.4. Server Protected by External Firewall Running NAT

In this case, the firewall must redirect traffic to the FTP server in addition to not blocking the required ports. For the sake of discussion, we will assume the FTP server in question is again the standard ftpd(8), using the default range of ports.

Here is an example subset of rules which would accomplish this:

```
ftp_server = "10.0.3.21"

rdr on $ext_if proto tcp from any to any \
    port 21 -> $ftp_server port 21
```

```
rdr on $ext_if proto tcp from any to any \
   port 49152:65535 -> $ftp_server port 49152:65535

 # in on $ext_if
pass in quick on $ext_if proto tcp from any \
   to $ftp_server port 21 keep state
pass in quick on $ext_if proto tcp from any \
   to $ftp_server port > 49151 keep state

 # out on $int_if
pass out quick on $int_if proto tcp from any \
   to $ftp_server port 21 keep state
pass out quick on $int_if proto tcp from any \
   to $ftp_server port > 49151 keep state
```

18. Authpf: User Shell for Authenticating Gateways

18.1. Overview

Authpf(8) is a user shell for authenticating gateways. An authenticating gateway is just like a regular network gateway (a.k.a. a router) except that users must first authenticate themselves to the gateway before it will allow traffic to pass through it. When a user's shell is set to /usr/sbin/authpf (i.e., instead of setting a user's shell to ksh or csh, for example) and the user logs in using SSH, authpf will make the necessary changes to the active pf(4) ruleset so that the user's traffic is passed through the filter and/or translated using Network Address Translation or redirection.

Once the user logs out or their session is disconnected, authpf will remove any rules loaded for the user and kill any stateful connections the user has open. Because of this, the ability of the user to pass traffic through the gateway only exists while the user keeps their SSH session open.

Authpf loads a user's filter and/or NAT rules into a unique anchor point. The anchor is named by combining the user's UNIX username and the authpf process-id into the format "username(PID)". Each user's anchor is stored within the authpf anchor which is in turn anchored to the main ruleset. The "fully qualified anchor path" then becomes:

main_ruleset/authpf/*username(PID)*

The rules that authpf loads can be configured on a per-user or global basis.

Example uses of authpf include:

- Requiring users to authenticate before allowing Internet access.

- Granting certain users – such as administrators – access to restricted parts of the network.

- Allowing only known users to access the rest of the network or Internet from a wireless network segment.

- Allowing workers from home or on the road access to resources on the company network. Users outside the office can not only open access to the company network, but can also be redirected to particular resources (e.g., their own desktop) based on the username they authenticate with.

- In a setting such as a library or other place with public Internet terminals, PF may be configured to allow limited Internet access to guest users. Authpf can then be used to provide registered users with complete access.

Authpf logs the username and IP address of each user who authenticates successfully as well as the start and end times of their login session via syslogd(8). By using this information, an administrator can determine who was logged in when and also make users accountable for their network traffic.

18.2. Configuring authpf

The basic steps needed to configure authpf are outlined here. For a complete description of authpf configuration, please refer to the authpf(8) man page.

Enabling Authpf

Authpf will not run if the config file /etc/authpf/authpf.conf is not present. Even if the file is empty (zero size), it must still be present or authpf will exit immediately after a user authenticates successfully.

The following configuration directives can be placed in authpf.conf:

- `anchor=name` - Use the specified anchor name instead of "authpf".

- `table=name` - Use the specified table name instead of "authpf_users".

On FreeBSD, authpf requires that a fdescfs(5) file system be mounted at /dev/fd before use. (Also see page 136.)

Linking Authpf into the Main Ruleset

Authpf is linked into the main ruleset by using anchor rules[1]:

```
nat-anchor "authpf/*"
rdr-anchor "authpf/*"
binat-anchor "authpf/*"
anchor "authpf/*"
```

Wherever the anchor rules are placed within the ruleset is where PF will branch off from the main ruleset to evaluate the authpf rules. It's not necessary for all four anchor rules to be present; for example, if authpf hasn't been setup to load any nat rules, the nat-anchor rule can be omitted.

Configuring Loaded Rules

Authpf loads its rules from one of two files:

- /etc/authpf/users/$USER/authpf.rules

- /etc/authpf/authpf.rules

The first file contains rules that are only loaded when the user $USER (which is replaced with the user's username) logs in. The per-user rule configuration is used when a specific user – such as an administrator – requires a set of rules that is different than the default set. The second file contains the default rules which are loaded for any user

---

[1]The authpf(8) manual page says the "/*" at the end of the anchor name is required to process the rulesets attached to the anchor.

that doesn't have their own authpf.rules file. If the user-specific file exists, it will override the default file. At least one of the files must exist or authpf will not run.

Filter and translation rules have the same syntax as in any other PF ruleset with one exception – Authpf allows for the use of two predefined macros:

- $user_ip - the IP address of the logged in user

- $user_id - the username of the logged in user

It's recommended practice to use the $user_ip macro to only permit traffic through the gateway from the authenticated user's computer.

In addition to the $user_ip macro, authpf will make use of the authpf_users table (if it exists) for storing the IP addresses of all authenticated users. Be sure to define the table before using it:

```
table <authpf_users> persist
pass in on $ext_if proto tcp from <authpf_users> \
    to port smtp flags S/SA keep state
```

This table should only be used in rules that are meant to apply to all authenticated users.

Access Control Lists

Users can be prevented from using authpf by creating a file in the /etc/authpf/banned/ directory and naming it after the username that is to be denied access. The contents of the file will be displayed to the user before authpf disconnects them. This provides a handy way to notify the user of why they're disallowed access and who to contact to have their access restored.

Conversely, it's also possible to allow only specific users access by placing usernames in the /etc/authpf/authpf.allow file. If the /etc/authpf/authpf.allow file does not exist or "*" is entered into the file, then authpf will permit access to any user who successfully logs in via SSH as long as they are not explicitly banned.

If authpf is unable to determine if a username is allowed or denied, it will print a brief message and then disconnect the user. An entry in

/etc/authpf/banned/ always overrides an entry in
/etc/authpf/authpf.allow.

Displaying a Login Message

Whenever a user successfully authenticates to authpf, a greeting is
printed that indicates that the user is authenticated.

```
Hello charlie. You are authenticated from host "64.59.56.140"
```

This message can be supplemented by putting a custom message in
/etc/authpf/authpf.message. The contents of this file will be displayed
after the default welcome message.

Assigning Authpf as a User's Shell

In order for authpf to work it must be assigned as the user's login
shell. When the user successfully authenticates to sshd(8), authpf will
be executed as the user's shell. It will then check if the user is allowed
to use authpf, load the rules from the appropriate file, etc.

There are a couple ways of assigning authpf as a user's shell:

1. Manually for each user using chsh(1), vipw(8), useradd(8),
   usermod(8), pw(8), etc.

2. By assigning users to a login class and changing the class's shell
   option in /etc/login.conf.

18.3. Creating an authpf Login Class

When using authpf on a system that has regular user accounts and authpf user accounts, it can be beneficial to create a separate login class
for the authpf users. This allows for certain changes to those accounts
to be made on a global basis and also allows different policies to be
placed on regular accounts and authpf accounts. Some examples of
what policies can be set:

- **shell** - Specify a user's login shell. This can be used to force a user's shell to authpf regardless of the entry in the passwd(5) database.

- **welcome** - Specify which motd(5) file to display when a user logs in. This is useful for displaying messages that are relevant only to authpf users.

Login classes are created in the login.conf(5) file. An example login class for authpf users:

```
authpf:\
    :welcome=/etc/motd.authpf:\
    :shell=/usr/sbin/authpf:\
    :tc=default:
```

Users are assigned to a login class by editing the class field of the user's master.passwd(5) database entry. One way to do this is with the chsh(1) command (when ran as the superuser).

18.4. Seeing Who is Logged In

Once a user has successfully logged in and authpf has adjusted the PF rules, authpf changes its process title to indicate the username and IP address of the logged in user:

```
# ps -ax | grep authpf
    23664 p0  Is+     0:00.11 -authpf: \
    charlie@192.168.1.3 (authpf)
```

Here the user charlie is logged in from the machine 192.168.1.3. By sending a SIGTERM signal to the authpf process, the user can be forcefully logged out. Authpf will also remove any rules loaded for the user and kill any stateful connections the user has open.

```
# kill -TERM 23664
```

18.5. Example

Authpf is being used on a BSD gateway to authenticate users on a wireless network which is part of a larger campus network. Once a user has authenticated, assuming they're not on the banned list, they will be permitted to SSH out and to browse the web (including secure websites) in addition to accessing either of the campus DNS servers.

The /etc/authpf/authpf.rules file contains the following rules:

```
wifi_if = "wi0"

pass in quick on $wifi_if proto tcp from $user_ip to \
    port { ssh, http, https } flags S/SA keep state
```

The administrative user charlie needs to be able to access the campus SMTP and POP3 servers in addition to surfing the web and using SSH. The following rules are setup in /etc/authpf/users/charlie/authpf.rules:

```
wifi_if = "wi0"
smtp_server = "10.0.1.50"
pop3_server = "10.0.1.51"

pass in quick on $wifi_if proto tcp from $user_ip \
    to $smtp_server port smtp flags S/SA keep state
pass in quick on $wifi_if proto tcp from $user_ip \
    to $pop3_server port pop3 flags S/SA keep state
pass in quick on $wifi_if proto tcp from $user_ip \
    to port { ssh, http, https } flags S/SA keep state
```

The main ruleset – located in /etc/pf.conf – is setup as follows:

```
# macros
wifi_if = "wi0"
ext_if  = "fxp0"
dns_servers = "{ 10.0.1.56, 10.0.2.56 }"

table <authpf_users> persist
```

```
scrub in all

# filter
block drop all

pass out quick on $ext_if inet proto tcp from \
   { $wifi_if:network, $ext_if } flags S/SA \
   modulate state
pass out quick on $ext_if inet proto { udp, icmp } \
   from { $wifi_if:network, $ext_if } keep state

pass in quick on $wifi_if inet proto tcp \
   from $wifi_if:network to $wifi_if \
   port ssh flags S/SA keep state

pass in quick on $wifi_if inet proto { tcp, udp } \
   from <authpf_users> \
   to $dns_servers port domain keep state
anchor "authpf/*" in on $wifi_if
```

The ruleset is very simple and does the following:

- Block everything (default deny).

- Pass outgoing TCP, UDP, and ICMP traffic on the external interface from the wireless network and from the gateway itself.

- Pass incoming SSH traffic from the wireless network destined
  for the gateway itself. This rule is necessary to permit users to
  log in.

- Pass incoming DNS requests from all authenticated authpf
  users to the campus DNS servers.

- Create the anchor point "authpf" for incoming traffic on the
  wireless interface.

The idea behind the main ruleset is to block everything and allow
the least amount of traffic through as possible. Traffic is free to flow

out on the external interface but is blocked from entering the wireless interface by the default deny policy. Once a user authenticates, their traffic is permitted to pass in on the wireless interface and to then flow through the gateway into the rest of the network. The quick keyword is used throughout so that PF doesn't have to evaluate each named ruleset when a new connection passes through the gateway.

19. Limiting spam with spamd

19.1. Overview

spamd is a small network daemon that pretends to know basic SMTP with the goal of wasting spammer resources. It does not queue email and can be used as a SMTP tarpit, as a greylisting[1] server, or to build blacklists.

The main usage is for your PF packet filter to redirect TCP port 25 (SMTP) connections to the port that spamd is listening on. PF tables are used to force connections to spamd or to your real SMTP server (like postfix).

The spamd suite comes with a few programs:

spamd - the mail deferral daemon.

spamd-setup - an optional tool for configuring spamd.

spamlogd - watches pflog(4) entries to create spamd whitelists.

spamdb - simple tool for manually adding or removing entries from the spamd database.

Only spamd (and pfctl) is needed for basic spamd (or greylisting) usage.

SpamAssassin also provides an unrelated program called "spamd," but it has different usage and purpose. SpamAssassin runs a large number of tests over a message – while spamd works on the level of connections between mail servers, and in fact, doesn't care about the contents of the messages. OpenBSD's spamd is a very effective tool for fighting spam, and considerably cheaper than SpamAssassin in terms of resources (CPU time, memory, clock time) used.

---

[1]Greylisting is covered in section 19.5.

This chapter is a quick introduction to the spamd suite. For more information, read the man pages for these tools.

19.2. Enabling spamd

To use spamd, make sure you have a /var/empty directory[2] and also a _spamd user and a _spamd group. At startup, the spamd daemon chroots to this empty directory and loses its root privileges.

Also make sure the default spamd TCP ports are listed in your service name database, for example in /etc/services:

```
spamd            8025/tcp      # spamd(8)
spamd-cfg        8026/tcp      # spamd(8) configuration
```

The spamd-cfg port is used with the optional spamd-setup utility covered in section 19.8.

Installing spamd on FreeBSD

spamd can be installed on FreeBSD by using the spamd package or by building the mail/spamd port.[3]

On FreeBSD systems, in order to use greylisting and update the PF tables, you need a file-descriptor file system, fdescfs(5), mounted at /dev/fd. You may need either a custom kernel or kldload the fdescfs kernel module. Mounting at boot time can be done by adding the following to /etc/fstab:

```
fdescfs /dev/fd fdescfs rw 0 0
```

On FreeBSD, the rc.d startup script is called pf-spamd.sh and to enable spamd at boot time add the following line to your /etc/rc.local:

```
pfspamd_enable=YES
```

Command-line arguments for spamd can be set on FreeBSD with the pfspamd_flags rc.conf variable.

---

[2]The spamd package from pkgsrc uses the /var/chroot/spamd directory instead.

[3]The FreeBSD spamd port can also be compiled to support the FreeBSD IPFW firewall instead of PF.

Installing spamd on NetBSD and DragonFly

Both NetBSD and DragonFly can install spamd using pkgsrc/mail/spamd or from a pre-built package for your system.

By default, this will install a /usr/pkg/etc/spamd.conf file for spamd-setup. The example configuration can also be found at /usr/pkg/share/examples/spamd/spamd.conf.

The pkgsrc package provides a rc.d startup script called pfspamd and the spamd daemon can be started at boot time on your NetBSD or DragonFly system by setting the following in your /etc/rc.conf:

```
pfspamd=YES
```

And spamd command-line arguments can be set with pfspamd_flags, such as:

```
pfspamd_flags="-s 10"
```

spamd and OpenBSD

OpenBSD has the spamd suite installed by default. To start spamd at boot on a OpenBSD system, set the following in the /etc/rc.conf.local file:

```
spamd_flags=""
```

spamd can be manually started by the superuser by running /usr/libexec/spamd (or /usr/local/libexec/spamd on FreeBSD or /usr/pkg/libexec/spamd on DragonFly and NetBSD).

19.3. spamd and PF

Simply use PF to redirect SMTP (port 25) connections to your spamd service.

The following pf.conf configuration defines a table called "spamd" (which exists even if empty) and then redirects SMTP traffic from addresses listed in the <spamd> table to your local spamd service running on your localhost at port 8025.

```
table <spamd> persist
rdr pass inet proto tcp from <spamd> to any \
    port smtp -> 127.0.0.1 port spamd
```

Then you can populate this <spamd> table with the IP addresses of
bad mail senders using pfctl, for example:

```
# pfctl -t spamd -T replace -f /etc/spammers
```

Or the spamd-setup tool covered in section 19.8 can do this for you.
If you want to tarpit all in-bound email, just use instead:

```
rdr pass inet proto tcp from any to any \
    port smtp -> 127.0.0.1 port spamd
```

A tarpit can also be created without PF by simply starting spamd on
the standard SMTP port 25 using the "-p" switch, for example:

```
# /usr/libexec/spamd -p 25
```

Or if you want to limit spam with PF without using spamd, see sections 5.2 and 5.3.

For more examples of implementing spamd with PF, see section
14.4.

19.4. Example SMTP Session

The following is an example SMTP session with spamd:

```
220 spamd.example.org ESMTP spamd IP-based SPAM blocker;
Tue Aug  1 12:49:20 2006
HELO localhost
250 Hello, spam sender. Pleased to be wasting your time.
MAIL FROM: <jeremy@example.org>
250 You are about to try to deliver spam. Your time will
be spent, for nothing.
RCPT TO: <someone@example.org>
```

```
250 This is hurting you more than it is hurting me.
DATA
354 Enter spam, end with "." on a line by itself
Subject: hello

What's up?
.
451 Temporary failure, please try again later.
```

The SMTP server response lines were sent very slow at one character per second (by default). In the above example, the characters in bold (including the period) were sent by the client. Notice that the sending server will send the entire message (such as a spam email) before it is rejected.

The 2xx lines are successful, the 3xx is informational and the 4xx is a temporary SMTP error. A legitimate, properly-configured MTA (mail transfer agent) will attempt to send the email again at a later time.

The spamd server closed the connection after sending the temporary error, 451.

The entire example session took over 13 minutes as logged in /var/log/messages:

```
Aug 1 12:49:20 glacier spamd[6815]: 127.0.0.1:
  connected (1/0)
Aug 1 13:02:33 glacier spamd[6815]: 127.0.0.1:
  disconnected after 793 seconds.
```

The time delay between sent characters can be adjusted with the -s option, such as five seconds per character: "-s 5". Turning off the delay can be done with "-s 0".

Also the socket receive buffer used during the SMTP DATA phase can be tuned to further slow down the spammer. Use the "-w" command line option to set the number of bytes for this window size. (The default may be 32768, but it depends on your system not spamd.)

The "-n" option can be used to define a different SMTP server greeting name. (The default as shown in the example is "spamd IP-based SPAM blocker".)

19.5. Greylisting with spamd

Greylisting is a useful spam prevention technique. Often spammers do not resend their spam when they receive a temporary error, while a legitimate MTA would retry later. This greylisting implementation refuses emails with a temporary SMTP error code until the IP of the sending mail system is whitelisted.

spamd records the initial connection's IP address and the envelope sender (MAIL FROM) and recipient (RCPT TO) in a Berkeley DB Btree database (normally at /var/db/spamd). If a connection after 25 minutes has these same details, then spamd will whitelist it in the same database.

Every minute[4], spamd will check the database and use pfctl to configure a PF table called <spamd-white>.

Note that other greylisting implementations usually accept the second valid SMTP connection, but with this spamd setup, the real mail server will not see the SMTP connection until the third attempt.

The database entry will be removed if four hours have passed and has not been retried. And whitelist (successful) database entries are removed after 864 hours (or about 36 days).

The greylisting feature is enabled with the "-g" command line option. It can be started at boot time on NetBSD, DragonFly, or FreeBSD by setting the following in /etc/rc.conf:

```
pfspamd_flags="-g"
```

Or on OpenBSD, set the following in /etc/rc.conf.local:

```
spamd_grey=YES
```

The time settings can be configured with the -G command line option, which defaults to "-G 25:4:864"; see the spamd(8) man page for more details.

---

[4]This is not configurable, except by recompiling spamd after modifying DB_SCAN_INTERVAL definition in grey.h.

19.5.1. PF Setup for Greylisting

PF is configured to redirect mail connections based on a PF table used by spamd, called "spamd-white". For example:

```
table <spamd-white> persist

rdr pass on xennet0 proto tcp from !<spamd-white> \
    to port smtp -> 127.0.0.1 port spamd
```

In the above example, a table called <spamd-white> is created and any SMTP connections on the xennet0 interface that are not listed in this <spamd-white> database are redirected to the spamd service.

Because the spamd daemon was started with the "-g" switch, the <spamd-white> table is automatically maintained as described above.

19.6. Maintaining the spamd Database

The spamdb tool can be used to maintain the spamdb database. It is not used to immediately update the <spamd-white> PF table.

The types of data in the database are SPAMTRAP, TRAPPED, WHITE, and GREY entries.[5] The WHITE entry is for IPs to be accepted (and this should correspond with the PF <spamd-white> table). The GREY entry is for the attempting host – during the greylisting phase.

Running "spamdb" by itself will display the entries in the database, delimited with a vertical bar. An example output of three records follows:

```
GREY|219.84.60.50|<npwfjvz@thief.com>|<reed@example.com>|
    1143704835|1143719235|1143719235|1|0
GREY|136.142.137.216|<survey@chasebank.com>|<pr@example.com>|
    1144146619|1144161019|1144161019|1|0
WHITE|220.150.229.248|||1143705152|1143707031|1146817454|2|0
```

The first column is the type. The second column is the sending host. The third field is the email address of the sender. The fourth field is

---

[5]SPAMTRAP and TRAPPED are covered in section 19.7.

the recipient email address. (Note that the whitelisted entry doesn't have the email addresses.)

The fifth, sixth and seventh fields are for the Unix time when this entry was first known, when it was last seen or when greylisted, and when it will expire from the database. On BSD systems, the "date -r" command can be used to view the Unix timestamps in a understandable format, for example:

```
$ date -r 1143704835
Thu Mar 30 01:47:15 CST 2006
```

The eighth column is the count of temporarily failed connections (for this entry). The final (ninth) field is the count of connections that have actually been sent to a real SMTP server – this is handled by spamlogd (covered in section 19.10).

To add an IP to the database, use the "-a" switch, like:

```
spamdb -a 71.247.126.240
```

This will add an entry of the "WHITE" type.

To remove an IP from the database use the "-d" switch followed by the IP.

As mentioned on page 140, the spamd daemon uses this database to update the PF <spamd-white> table.

The pfctl tool can be used to review the <spamd-white> table, for example to lists the IPs in the table use:

```
pfctl -t spamd-white -T show
```

Normally pfctl would not be used to modify the table since it is maintained by spamd.

19.7. Greytrapping

With greytrapping, bogus or old unused email addresses are used as traps for spammers. When a host – that is not whitelisted – attempts to send to the spamtrap address, it is temporarily blacklisted by spamd for 24 hours.

The greytrapping feature is only enabled when spamd is started with the "-g" command line option (as covered in section 19.5.)

The spamdb tool is used to assign these spamtrap addresses, for example:

```
# spamdb -T -a "<fun@reedmedia.net>"
```

Note that the address includes the brackets as normally used in the SMTP RCPT TO dialog.

In the spamdb database, the addresses are identified as SPAM-TRAP. And the bad hosts that tried to mail to the SPAMTRAP addresses are identified with TRAPPED. For example:

```
# spamdb  | grep TRAP
TRAPPED|212.216.176.224|1155909525
SPAMTRAP|<fun@reedmedia.net>
```

The third field for the TRAPPED entry is the expiration time (24 hours after their attempt).

You can manually add TRAPPED entries with spamdb also, for example:

```
spamdb -t -a 200.90.188.13
```

19.8. The spamd configuration

As explained earlier, PF is used to control redirection to spamd based on a single whitelist or blacklist entry. The following is pf.conf example that includes using both the whitelist and blacklist:

```
table <spamd> persist
table <spamd-white> persist

rdr pass on $ext_if proto tcp from <spamd> \
    to port smtp -> 127.0.0.1 port spamd

rdr pass on $ext_if proto tcp from !<spamd-white> \
    to port smtp -> 127.0.0.1 port spamd
```

The spamd-setup tool is an optional utility for maintaining the <spamd> PF table containing a blacklist. The spamd daemon can have multiple lists with different deferral messages which is also configured by spamd-setup. (The default deferral message is "Temporary failure, please try again later.")

spamd.conf

spam-setup uses a spamd.conf file which is based on the capability database format. It must contain at least one capability record named "all". This record lists the blacklists and whitelists in the order they should be applied. These whitelists and blacklists are defined in other records. The capabilities are:

black blacklist type

white whitelist type used to override previous blacklist entries.

msg custom deferral message; this is either a path to a file to read, or if in quotes, the message itself.

method source of list, either http://, ftp://, a file, or "exec" for the output of a command.

file depending on the method, this is a URL (without the URI:// part), a path to a file to load, or a path to a program to run.

The default spamd.conf file contains several examples of block lists. The following are the default records used by spamd-setup. (Review the complete spamd.conf file for more examples.)

```
all:\
    :spews1:china:korea:

# Mirrored from http://www.spews.org/spews_list_level1.txt
spews1:\
    :black:\
    :msg="SPAM. Your address %A is in the spews \
    level 1 database\n\
    See http://www.spews.org/ask.cgi?x=%A for \
    more details":\
```

```
        :method=http:\
        :file=www.openbsd.org/spamd/spews_list_level1.txt.gz:

# Mirrored from http://www.okean.com/chinacidr.txt
china:\
        :black:\
        :msg="SPAM. Your address %A appears to be from China\n\
        See http://www.okean.com/asianspamblocks.html for \
        more details":\
        :method=http:\
        :file=www.openbsd.org/spamd/chinacidr.txt.gz:

# Mirrored from http://www.okean.com/koreacidr.txt
korea:\
        :black:\
        :msg="SPAM. Your address %A appears to be from Korea\n\
        See http://www.okean.com/asianspamblocks.html for \
        more details":\
        :method=http:\
        :file=www.openbsd.org/spamd/koreacidr.txt.gz:
```

In addition to the spamd.conf(5) manual page, the cgetcap(3) manual page also describes the format of the configuration file.

spamd-setup sorts, removes overlapping entries, removes whitelists entries, and also simplifies the blacklist by creating CIDR net blocks as applicable.

Then spamd-setup connects to spamd on the loopback interface on the spamd-cfg TCP port to provide its processed blacklist configuration to spamd. It also runs pfctl to update the <spamd> PF table.

spamd-setup can be ran at system boot up or via cron as needed.

Note that spamd-setup is not needed for basic spamd usage.

19.9. Bypassing spamd

The spamd service can be bypassed with PF by using the <spamd-white> as described earlier or by using another PF table. The whitelists that can be defined using spamd.conf are only used for overriding the <spamd> blacklist created by spamd-setup. The following is a pf.conf example of creating a permanent or custom whitelist to always bypass the spam deferral daemon:

```
table <spamd-pass> persist file "/etc/spamd-whitelist"

no rdr pass on $ext_if proto tcp from <spamd-pass> \
    to port smtp
```

PF would load the file containing IPs of good hosts to accept mail from. And the "no rdr" rule excludes any redirection for mailers coming from that table.

This would be followed by the the redirect (rdr) rules for <spamd-white> and/or <spamd> as shown in section 19.8.

The pfctl tool can be used to maintain this <spamd-pass> table.

List IPs in table:

```
pfctl -t spamd-pass -T show
```

Adding IP (or multiple IPs) to table:

```
pfctl -t spamd-pass -T add 172.16.9.41
```

Removing IP(s) from table:

```
pfctl -t spamd-pass -T delete 192.168.10.39
```

Reload table from file:

```
pfctl -t spamd-pass -T replace -f /etc/spamd-whitelist
```

The "add" and "delete" syntax allows multiple IPs to be added or removed on the same command line. See chapter 5 for more information about PF tables.

19.10. Auto whitelists with spamlogd

Whitelist database entries can be updated or added by spamlogd. It does not directly update the PF table – spamd checks the spamdb database and updates the <spamd-white> PF table. The optional spamlogd daemon runs tcpdump to watch for SMTP connections:

```
tcpdump -l -n -e -i pflog0 -q -t port 25 and \
       action pass and "tcp[13]&0x12=0x2"
```

Note that pflog(4) is used and your real port 25 traffic must be logged[6] by PF to be used by spamlogd. In the following pf.conf example, "ne1" is the external interface and 172.16.2.3 is the mail server.

```
pass in log on ne1 proto tcp to 172.16.2.3 \
     port smtp keep state
pass out log on ne1 proto tcp from 172.16.2.3 \
     to port smtp keep state
```

Then spamlogd adds (or updates) the source address for inbound traffic as a whitelist entry. And for outbound traffic, it adds the destination address to the whitelist with the assumption that a legitimate email reply may come back from that address. This is useful so that any replies to outbound email will not be delayed by greylisting. The "-I" command-line switch can be used to turn off the whitelisting of outbound SMTP connections.

---

[6]The pflogd daemon is not needed. For more information about PF logging, see chapter 15.

20. Firewall Redundancy with CARP and pfsync

20.1. Introduction to CARP

CARP is the Common Address Redundancy Protocol. Its primary purpose is to allow multiple hosts on the same network segment to share an IP address (to provide high availability). CARP is a secure, free alternative to the Virtual Router Redundancy Protocol (VRRP)[1] and the Hot Standby Router Protocol (HSRP)[2]. CARP was designed and implemented by OpenBSD starting in 2003.

CARP works by allowing a group of hosts on the same network segment to share an IP address. This group of hosts is referred to as a "redundancy group". The redundancy group is assigned an IP address that is shared amongst the group members. Within the group, one host is designated the "master" and the rest as "backups". The master host is the one that currently "holds" the shared IP; it responds to any traffic or ARP requests directed towards it. Each host may belong to more than one redundancy group at a time.

One common use for CARP is to create a group of redundant firewalls. The virtual IP that is assigned to the redundancy group is configured on client machines as the default gateway. In the event that the master firewall suffers a failure or is taken offline, the IP will move to one of the backup firewalls and service will continue unaffected.

CARP supports IPv4 and IPv6.

---

[1] http://www.ietf.org/rfc/rfc3768.txt
[2] http://www.ietf.org/rfc/rfc2281.txt

20.2. CARP Operation

The master host in the group sends regular advertisements to the local network so that the backup hosts know it's still alive. If the backup hosts don't hear an advertisement from the master for a set period of time, then one of them will take over the duties of master (whichever backup host has the lowest configured `advbase` and `advskew` values).

It's possible for multiple CARP groups to exist on the same network segment. CARP advertisements contain the Virtual Host ID which allows group members to identify which redundancy group the advertisement belongs to.

In order to prevent a malicious user on the network segment from spoofing CARP advertisements, each group can be configured with a password. Each CARP packet sent to the group is then protected by SHA1-HMAC cryptography.

Since CARP is its own protocol it should have an explicit pass rule in filter rulesets:

```
pass out on $carp_dev proto carp keep state
```

The `$carp_dev` macro should be the physical interface that CARP is communicating over.

20.3. Configuring CARP on FreeBSD and OpenBSD

Each redundancy group is represented by a carp(4) virtual network interface. As such, CARP is configured using ifconfig(8) on OpenBSD, NetBSD, and FreeBSD.

```
ifconfig carpN create

ifconfig carpN vhid vhid [pass password] \
    [carpdev carpdev] [advbase advbase] \
    [advskew advskew] [state state] \
    ipaddress mask
```

carpN The name of the carp(4) virtual interface where *N* is an integer that represents the interface's number (e.g. carp10).

vhid The Virtual Host ID. This is a unique number that is used to identify the redundancy group to other nodes on the network. Acceptable values are from 1 to 255.

password The authentication password to use when talking to other CARP-enabled hosts in this redundancy group. This must be the same on all members of the group.

carpdev This optional parameter specifies the physical network interface to be used by the carp(4) pseudo-device. This allows using an IP-less physical interface. By default, CARP will try to determine which interface to use by looking for a physical interface that is in the same subnet as the *ipaddress* and *mask* combination given to the carp(4) interface. FreeBSD does not have this ifconfig "carpdev" feature. This was introduced in OpenBSD 3.7.

advbase This optional parameter specifies how often, in seconds, to advertise that we're a member of the redundancy group. The default is 1 second. Acceptable values are from 1 to 255.

advskew This optional parameter specifies how much to skew the *advbase* when sending CARP advertisements. By manipulating *advbase*, the master CARP host can be chosen. The higher the number, the *less* preferred the host will be when choosing a master. The default is 0. Acceptable values are from 1 to 254.

state Force a carp(4) interface into a certain state. Valid states are init, backup, and master. FreeBSD does not have this ifconfig "state" parameter and does not allow the state of a carp interface to be changed explicitly. This was introduced in OpenBSD 3.5.

ipaddress This is the shared IP address assigned to the redundancy group. This address does not have to be in the same subnet as the IP address on the physical interface (if present). This address needs to be the same on all hosts in the group, however.

mask The subnet mask of the shared IP.

Further CARP behavior can be controlled via sysctl(8):

net.inet.carp.allow Accept incoming CARP packets or not. Default is 1 (yes).

net.inet.carp.preempt Allow hosts within a redundancy group that have a have a high advertisement frequency (better advbase and advskew) to preempt the master. In addition, this option also enables failing over all interfaces in the event that one interface goes down. If one physical CARP-enabled interface goes down, CARP will change advskew to 240 on all other CARP-enabled interfaces, in essence, failing itself over. This option is 0 (disabled) by default.

net.inet.carp.log Log bad CARP packets. Default is 0 (disabled).

net.inet.carp.arpbalance Load balance traffic across multiple redundancy group hosts. Default is 0 (disabled). See the carp(4) manual page for more information.

20.4. carp(4) Example

Here is an example CARP configuration on OpenBSD:

```
# sysctl -w net.inet.carp.allow=1
# ifconfig carp1 create
# ifconfig carp1 vhid 1 pass mekmitasdigoat \
    carpdev em0 advskew 100 10.0.0.1 255.255.255.0
```

This sets up the following:

- Enables receipt of CARP packets (this is the default setting).

- Creates a carp(4) interface, named "carp1".

- Configures carp1 for virtual host #1, enables a password, sets em0 as the interface to be used by carp1[3], and makes this host a backup due to the advskew of 100 (assuming of course that the master is set up with an advskew less than 100). The shared IP assigned to this group is 10.0.0.1/255.255.255.0.

Running ifconfig on carp1 shows the status of the interface.

```
# ifconfig carp1
carp1: flags=8802<UP,BROADCAST,SIMPLEX,MULTICAST> mtu 1500
        carp: BACKUP carpdev em0 vhid 1 advbase 1 advskew 100
        inet 10.0.0.1 netmask 0xffffff00 broadcast 10.0.0.255
```

20.5. Introduction to pfsync

The pfsync(4) network interface exposes certain changes made to the pf(4) state table. By monitoring this device using tcpdump, state table changes can be observed in real time. In addition, the pfsync(4) interface can send these state change messages out on the network so that other nodes running PF can merge the changes into their own state tables. Likewise, pfsync(4) can also listen on the network for incoming messages.

Note that some different versions of pfsync can sometimes not keep state with each other.

20.6. pfsync Operation

By default, pfsync(4) does not send or receive state table updates on the network; however, updates can still be monitored using tcpdump or other such tools on the local machine.

When pfsync(4) is set up to send and receive updates on the network, the default behavior is to multicast updates out on the local network. All updates are sent without authentication.[4] Best common practice is either:

---

[3]The carpdev feature was introduced in OpenBSD 3.7.

[4]According to the pfsync(4) manual page, it would be trivial to spoof packets which create states, bypassing the PF ruleset. Use a trusted network with pfsync!

1. Connect the two nodes that will be exchanging updates back-to-back using a crossover cable and use that interface as the syncdev.

2. Use the ifconfig(8) syncpeer option so that updates are unicast directly to the peer, then configure ipsec(4) between the hosts to secure the pfsync(4) traffic.

When updates are being sent and received on the network, pfsync packets should be passed in the filter ruleset:

```
pass on $sync_if proto pfsync
```

The `$sync_if` macro should be the physical interface that pfsync(4) is communicating over.

20.7. Configuring pfsync

Since pfsync(4) is a virtual network interface, it is configured using ifconfig(8).

```
ifconfig pfsyncN syncdev syncdev \
   [syncpeer syncpeer]
```

pfsyncN The name of the pfsync(4) interface. pfsync0 exists by default when using the GENERIC kernel.

syncdev The name of the physical interface used to send pfsync updates out.

syncpeer This optional parameter specifies the IP address of a host to exchange pfsync updates with. By default, pfsync updates are multicast on the local network. This option overrides that behavior and instead unicasts the update to the specified *syncpeer*.

Note that the synchronization interface needs to be up and have an IP address assigned.

20.8. pfsync Example

Here is an example pfsync configuration:

```
# ifconfig pfsync0 syncdev em1
```

This enables pfsync on the em1 interface. Outgoing updates will be multicast on the network allowing any other host running pfsync to receive them.

20.9. Combining CARP and pfsync For Failover

By combining the features of CARP and pfsync, a group of two or more firewalls can be used to create a highly-available, fully-redundant firewall cluster. As explained earlier, CARP handles the automatic failover of one firewall to another and pfsync synchronizes the state table amongst all the firewalls. In the event of a failover, traffic can flow uninterrupted through the new master firewall.

An example scenario follows with two firewalls, fw1 and fw2.

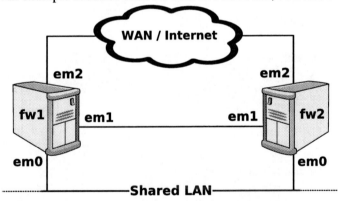

The firewalls are connected back-to-back using a crossover cable on em1. Both are connected to the LAN on em0 and to a WAN/Internet connection on em2. IP addresses are as follows:

- fw1 em0: 172.16.0.1

- fw1 em1: 10.10.10.1

- fw1 em2: 192.0.2.1

- fw2 em0: 172.16.0.2

- fw2 em1: 10.10.10.2

- fw2 em2: 192.0.2.2

- LAN shared IP: 172.16.0.100

- WAN/Internet shared IP: 192.0.2.100

The network policy is that fw1 will be the preferred master.

Configure fw1:

Enable preemption and group interface failover:

```
# sysctl -w net.inet.carp.preempt=1
```

Configure pfsync:

```
# ifconfig em1 10.10.10.1 netmask 255.255.255.0
# ifconfig pfsync0 syncdev em1
# ifconfig pfsync0 up
```

Configure CARP on the LAN side:

```
# ifconfig carp1 create
# ifconfig carp1 vhid 1 carpdev em0 pass lanpasswd \
      172.16.0.100 255.255.255.0
```

Configure CARP on the WAN/Internet side:

```
# ifconfig carp2 create
# ifconfig carp2 vhid 2 carpdev em2 pass netpasswd \
      192.0.2.100 255.255.255.0
```

Configure fw2:

Enable preemption and group interface failover:

```
# sysctl -w net.inet.carp.preempt=1
```

Configure pfsync:

```
# ifconfig em1 10.10.10.2 netmask 255.255.255.0
# ifconfig pfsync0 syncdev em1
# ifconfig pfsync0 up
```

Configure CARP on the LAN side:

```
# ifconfig carp1 create
# ifconfig carp1 vhid 1 carpdev em0 pass lanpasswd \
    advskew 128 172.16.0.100 255.255.255.0
```

Configure CARP on the WAN/Internet side:

```
# ifconfig carp2 create
# ifconfig carp2 vhid 2 carpdev em2 pass netpasswd \
    advskew 128 192.0.2.100 255.255.255.0
```

20.10. Operational Issues

The following are some common operational issues encountered with CARP and pfsync.

Configuring CARP and pfsync During Boot

Since carp(4) and pfsync(4) are both types of network interfaces, they can be configured at boot on OpenBSD by creating a hostname.if(5) file. The netstart startup script will take care of creating the interface and configuring it. Here are some OpenBSD examples:

/etc/hostname.carp1

```
inet 172.16.0.100 255.255.255.0 172.16.0.255 \
    vhid 1 carpdev em0 pass lanpasswd
```

/etc/hostname.pfsync0

```
up syncdev em1
```

On NetBSD, carp(4) is also a type of network interface and can be enabled by creating an ifconfig.carpXX file in /etc, or in rc.conf. (See the rc.conf(5) and ifconfig.if(5) manual pages for details.)

Forcing Failover of the Master

There can be times when it's necessary to failover or demote the master node on purpose. Examples include taking the master node down for maintenance or when troubleshooting a problem. The objective here is to gracefully failover traffic to one of the backup hosts so that users do not notice any impact.

To failover, shut down the carp(4) interface on the master node.

```
# ifconfig carp1 down
```

This will cause the master to advertise itself with an "infinite" advbase and advskew. The backup host(s) will see this and immediately take over the role of master.

Ruleset Tips

Filter the physical interface. As far as PF is concerned, network traffic comes from the physical interface, not the CARP virtual interface (i.e., carp0). So, write your rule sets accordingly. Don't forget that an interface name in a PF rule can be either the name of a physical interface or an address associated with that interface. For example, this rule could be correct:

```
pass in on fxp0 inet proto tcp from any \
   to carp0 port 22
```

but replacing the fxp0 with carp0 would not work as you desire.

Don't forget to pass proto carp and proto pfsync!

21. Example Ruleset: Firewall for Home or Small Office

21.1. The Scenario

In this example, PF is running on a BSD machine acting as a firewall and NAT gateway for a small network in a home or office. The overall objective is to provide Internet access to the network and to allow limited access to the firewall machine from the Internet, and expose an internal web server to the external Internet. This chapter will go through a complete ruleset that does just that.

21.2. The Network

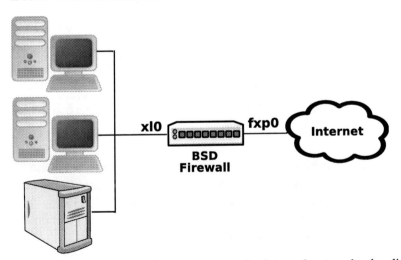

There are a number of computers on the internal network; the diagram above shows three but the actual number is irrelevant. These computers are regular workstations used for web surfing, email, chatting, etc., except for COMP3 which is also running a small web server.

The internal network is using the 192.168.0.0 / 255.255.255.0 network block.

The BSD firewall is a Celeron 300 with two network cards: a 3com 3c905B (xl0) and an Intel EtherExpress Pro/100 (fxp0). The firewall has a cable connection to the Internet and is using NAT to share this connection with the internal network. The IP address on the external interface is dynamically assigned by the Internet Service Provider.

21.3. The Objective

The objectives are:

- Provide unrestricted Internet access to each internal computer.

- Use a "default deny" filter ruleset.

- Allow the following incoming traffic to the firewall from the Internet:

    o SSH (TCP port 22): this will be used for external maintenance of the firewall machine.

    o Auth/Ident (TCP port 113): used by some services such as SMTP and IRC.

    o ICMP Echo Requests: the ICMP packet type used by ping.

- Redirect TCP port 80 connection attempts (which are attempts to access a web server) to computer COMP3. Also, permit TCP port 80 traffic destined for COMP3 through the firewall.

- Log filter statistics on the external interface.

- By default, reply with a TCP RST or ICMP Unreachable for blocked packets.

- Make the ruleset as simple and easy to maintain as possible.

Preparation

This example assumes that the BSD host has been properly configured to act as a router, including verifying IP networking setup, Internet connectivity, and setting sysctl(8) variable `net.inet.ip.forwarding` to "1". (See section 7.4 for more information.) It is likely you will also want to have activated PF in /etc/rc.conf or /etc/rc.conf.local.

21.4. The Ruleset

The following will step through a ruleset that will accomplish the above goals.

Macros

The following macros are defined to make maintenance and reading of the ruleset easier:

```
ext_if="fxp0"
int_if="xl0"

tcp_services="{ 22, 113 }"
icmp_types="echoreq"

comp3="192.168.0.3"
```

The first two lines define the network interfaces that filtering will happen on. By defining them here, if we have to move this system to another machine with different hardware, we can change only those two lines, and the rest of the rule set will be still usable. The third and fourth lines list the TCP port numbers of the services that will be opened up to the Internet (SSH and ident/auth) and the ICMP packet types that will be accepted at the firewall machine. Finally, the last line defines the IP address of COMP3.

Note: If the Internet connection required PPPoE, then filtering and NAT would have to take place on the tun0 interface and *not* on fxp0.

Options

The following two options will set the default response for block filter rules and turn statistics logging "on" for the external interface:

```
set block-policy return
set loginterface $ext_if
```

Every Unix system has a "loopback" interface. It's a virtual network interface that is used by applications to talk to each other inside the system. On BSD systems, the loopback interface is lo(4). It is considered best practice to disable all filtering on loopback interfaces. Using set skip will accomplish this.

```
set skip on lo
```

Note that we are skipping the entire "lo" interface group; this way, should we later add additional loopback interfaces, we won't have to worry about altering this portion of our existing rules file.

The set skip feature was added in PF 3.7. For older versions of PF, in general, all traffic should be passed on the loopback interface:

```
pass quick on lo0 all
```

Scrub

There is no reason not to use the recommended scrubbing of all incoming traffic, so this is a simple one-liner:

```
scrub in
```

Network Address Translation

To perform NAT for the entire internal network the following nat rule is used:

```
nat on $ext_if from !($ext_if) to any -> ($ext_if)
```

The "!($ext_if)" could easily be replaced by a "$int_if" in this case, but if you added multiple internal interfaces, you would have to add additional NAT rules; whereas with this structure, NAT will be handled on all protected interfaces.

Since the IP address on the external interface is assigned dynamically, parentheses are placed around the translation interface so that PF will notice when the address changes.

As we will want to have the FTP proxy working, we'll put the NAT anchor in, too:

```
nat-anchor "ftp-proxy/*"
```

Redirection

The first redirection rules needed are for ftp-proxy(8) so that FTP clients on the local network can connect to FTP servers on the Internet.

```
rdr-anchor "ftp-proxy/*"
rdr on $int_if proto tcp from any \
    to any port 21 -> 127.0.0.1 port 8021
```

Note that this rule will only catch FTP connections to port 21. If users regularly connect to FTP servers on other ports, then a list should be used to specify the destination port, for example: from any to any port { 21, 2121 }.

The last redirection rule catches any attempts by someone on the Internet to connect to TCP port 80 on the firewall. Legitimate attempts to access this port will be from users trying to access the network's web server. These connection attempts need to be redirected to COMP3:

```
rdr on $ext_if proto tcp from any \
    to any port 80 -> $comp3
```

Filter Rules

Now the filter rules. Start with the default deny:

```
block in
```

At this point, all traffic attempting to come into an interface will be blocked, even that from the internal network. Later rules will open up the firewall as per the objectives above as well as open up any necessary virtual interfaces.

Keep in mind, pf can block traffic coming into or leaving out of an interface. It can simplify your life if you chose to filter traffic in one direction, rather than trying to keep it straight when filtering some things in, and some things out. In our case, we'll opt to filter the inbound traffic, but once the traffic is permitted into an interface, we won't try to obstruct it leaving, so we will do the following:

```
pass out keep state
```

We need to have an anchor for ftp-proxy(8):

```
anchor "ftp-proxy/*"
```

It is good to use the spoofed address protection:

```
antispoof quick for { lo $int_if }
```

Now open the ports used by those network services that will be available to the Internet. First, the traffic that is destined to the firewall itself:

```
pass in on $ext_if inet proto tcp from any to \
   ($ext_if) port $tcp_services flags S/SA keep state
```

Specifying the network ports in the macro $tcp_services makes it simple to open additional services to the Internet by simply editing the macro and reloading the ruleset. UDP services can also be opened up by creating a $udp_services macro and adding a filter rule, similar to the one above, that specifies proto udp.

In addition to having an rdr rule which passes the web server traffic to COMP3, we must also pass this traffic through the firewall:

```
pass in on $ext_if inet proto tcp from any to $comp3 \
   port 80 flags S/SA synproxy state
```

For an added bit of safety, we'll make use of the TCP SYN Proxy to further protect the web server.

ICMP traffic needs to be passed:

```
pass in inet proto icmp all icmp-type $icmp_types \
  keep state
```

Similar to the $tcp_services macro, the $icmp_types macro can easily be edited to change the types of ICMP packets that will be allowed to reach the firewall. Note that this rule applies to all network interfaces.

Now traffic must be passed to and from the internal network. We'll assume that the users on the internal network know what they are doing and aren't going to be causing trouble. This is not necessarily a valid assumption; a much more restrictive ruleset would be appropriate for many environments.

```
pass in quick on $int_if
```

TCP, UDP, and ICMP traffic is permitted to exit the firewall towards the Internet due to the earlier "pass out keep state" line. State information is kept so that the returning packets will be passed in through the firewall.

21.5. The Complete Ruleset

```
# macros
ext_if="fxp0"
int_if="xl0"

tcp_services="{ 22, 113 }"
icmp_types="echoreq"

comp3="192.168.0.3"

# options
set block-policy return
```

```
set loginterface $ext_if

set skip on lo0

# scrub
scrub in

# nat/rdr
nat on $ext_if from !($ext_if) to any -> ($ext_if:0)
nat-anchor "ftp-proxy/*"
rdr-anchor "ftp-proxy/*"

rdr pass on $int_if proto tcp \
    to port ftp -> 127.0.0.1 port 8021
rdr on $ext_if proto tcp from any to any \
    port 80 -> $comp3

# filter rules
block in

pass out keep state

anchor "ftp-proxy/*"
antispoof quick for { lo $int_if }

pass in on $ext_if inet proto tcp from any \
    to ($ext_if) port $tcp_services \
    flags S/SA keep state

pass in on $ext_if inet proto tcp from any to $comp3 \
    port 80 flags S/SA synproxy state

pass in inet proto icmp all icmp-type $icmp_types \
    keep state

pass quick on $int_if
```

A. Other Tools

Various utilities related to PF are available for analyzing logs and stats, configuring rulesets, managing firewalls, and more. The following is a list of many of the available tools.

The Bridge Keeper

This dynamic firewall daemon framework helps set up and optionally maintain the packet filter.

http://www.lightconsulting.com/~travis/dfd/dfd_keeper/dfd_keeper/
http://www.lightconsulting.com/~travis/dfd/

BruteForceBlocker

This script checks sshd logs and counts number of "Failed Login" attempts. When an address reaches a configured limit, BruteForce-Blocker adds the IP to PF's table to block its traffic.

http://danger.rulez.sk/projects/bruteforceblocker/

Expiretable

Removes entries from the pf(4) table based on their age – the amount of time that has passed since the statistics for each entry in the target table was last cleared.

FreeBSD ports: security/expiretable
OpenBSD ports: sysutils/expiretable
http://expiretable.fnord.se/

fwanalog

fwanalog parses and summarizes firewall logfiles. It converts the logs to fake web server logs and runs the Analog web log analyzer with a modified configuration to generate the reports.

FreeBSD ports: security/fwanalog
http://tud.at/programm/fwanalog/

Firewall Builder

Firewall Builder is a multi-platform firewall configuration and management tool. It consists of a GUI and a set of policy compilers for various firewall platforms. Firewall Builder helps administrators maintain a database of network objects and services and allows policy editing using simple drag-and-drop operations.

FreeBSD ports: security/fwanalog
OpenBSD ports: security/fwbuilder
Pkgsrc: security/fwbuilder
http://www.fwbuilder.org/

Hatchet - PF Firewall Log Parser

Hatchet is a log parsing and viewing utility. It presents HTML output of logged events and utilization graphs. Hatchet archives the logs so that you can search past events. It also allows you to sort by column, so that you may isolate traffic by source or destination address, service, rule number, etc. Additionally, it provides external links to perform DNS queries on source addresses and service queries from SANS.

http://www.dixongroup.net/hatchet/

IPA

A flexible general purpose network accounting system that supports pf. It supports limits for accounting rules and limits events such as "limit is reached" and "reached limit is expired". It also understands time intervals such as "end of day", "end of week", and "end of month".

FreeBSD ports: sysutils/ipa
Pkgsrc: net/ipa
http://ipa-system.sourceforge.net/

Metacortex

Metacortex is a web-based graphical user interface and rule generator for PF. It can provide PF statistics, lists of active connections, log analysis, and various system statistics such as uptime and virtual memory stats.

http://www.securityoffice.net/products/metacortex/

P0f

P0f is a versatile passive OS fingerprinting tool which does not generate any additional network traffic and can not be detected. PF includes an OS fingerprinting implementation based on the p0f methodology and signature database. (P0f is not needed to use PF's operating system filtering; see section 6.13 for details.)

OpenBSD ports: security/p0f
Pkgsrc: security/p0f
http://lcamtuf.coredump.cx/p0f.shtml

pf2mrtg

Script to help enable monitoring of PF. It enables PF logging and gathers stats for various parameters to monitor and converts to four-column MRTG format which can be used to generate graphs.

https://www.solarflux.org/pf/pf2mrtg.sh.txt

pf2x

Command-line PHP Script takes the output of your pflog and converts into various different output formats: XML, HTML, plain text, PDF, MySQL INSERT statements, and PostgreSQL INSERT statements. It can also generate a statistics report in HTML and a 24-hour graph of the traffic (using rrdtool).

http://craz1.homelinux.com/#pf2x

pf_dns_lookup

This python script looks up DNS names and puts them in a PF table for you.

http://www.lightconsulting.com/~travis/pf_dns_lookup/

pfflowd

pfflowd converts PF state expiry messages (sent in realtime via the pfsync interface) to Cisco NetFlow datagrams which may be sent (via UDP) to a host.

FreeBSD ports: net/pfflowd
http://www.mindrot.org/pfflowd.html

pfpro

Java-based graphical interface for creating and maintaining firewall configurations. It uses XML which can be verified efficiently (by checking via DTD).

http://pfpro.sf.net/

pfSense

pfSense is a custom, small version of FreeBSD that provides a firewall system. It provides a web-based configuration and administration interface. It offers multiple WAN support, CARP clustering, ALTQ traffic shaping, upgrades through web-interface, DHCP client, NAT, PPTP, IPsec, and a lot more.

http://pfsense.org/

pfstat

Small utility that collects packet filter statistics and produces graphs.

FreeBSD ports: sysutils/pfstat
OpenBSD ports: net/pfstat
Pkgsrc: sysutils/pfstat
http://www.benzedrine.cx/pfstat.htm

PFsysinfo

Web-based frontend for reporting PF system information. It provides PF statistics for active connections and current ruleset; log analysis;

graphs with pfstat; and system status (processes, uptime, vmstat).

   http://team.gcu-squad.org/~aflab/projects/pfsysinfo/

pftop

A text-mode real-time display tool for active PF states. It also has rule
and queue pages, and can compute per state throughput.

   FreeBSD ports: sysutils/pftop
   OpenBSD ports: sysutils/pftop
   Pkgsrc: sysutils/pftop
   http://www.eee.metu.edu.tr/~canacar/pftop/

pfw

PHP-based web front-end to PF that allows managing remote firewalls and the local ruleset including editing macros, address translation, queues, scrub, tables, filter rules, and displaying realtime logs.

   FreeBSD ports: security/pfw
   http://www.allard.nu/pfw/

rpfcd

Remote PF control daemon allows remote control and monitoring of
PF. It communicates with clients using RPFC protocol running on
top of SSL (Secure Socket Layer). The protocol is designed to be
relatively forgiving and easy to use.

   http://www.insecure.dk/rpfcd

SASacct

Perl-based accounting package, used for collecting traffic statistics
from pfctl. CGI script is used to display graphs, weekly traffic stats
and bandwith utilization.

   http://rousse.pm.org/sasacct/

sessionlimit

Sessionlimit interacts with PF in order to contain the intruders activities after a compromise of a honeypot. It can detect when a scan or DoS is initiated from a honeypot. Then it can use PF to block any new outgoing connections. It can also expire the blocks (such as after 1800 seconds). It logs its work via syslog.

http://www.honeynet.org.br/tools/#sessionlimit

snort2c

snort2c analyzes Snort's alertfile output and blocks attackers using PF. You can have a whitelist for protected hosts. It also provides a tool to display the IPs blocked by snort2c. It will log via syslog.

http://snort2c.sourceforge.net/

snort2pf

Perl daemon which greps the Snort alertfile and blocks the IP addresses of attackers for a given span of time.

https://snort2pf.unixgu.ru/

SnortSam

A plug-in for the Snort Intrusion Detection System for automated and distributed blocking of IP addresses using PF (and various other firewalls). It provides whitelist support and it can share block requests with other systems.

http://www.snortsam.net/

spamd

This is covered in chapter 19.

spamd is a simple SMTP service tarpit designed to reject emails and waste the time and resources of a spam sender. PF can be used to redirect all mail connections to this daemon. It includes a tool to configure blacklists and whitelists with corresponding pf(4) table entries, and a tool to list, remove or add entries in the spamdb database.

Spamd also provides a greylisting mode which can automatically up-date the pf(4) tables. It is maintained by the OpenBSD project and is included with the default installation of OpenBSD.

FreeBSD port: mail/spamd

Pkgsrc: mail/spamd

sshit

This Perl script uses PF to block IP addresses that generate too many failed login attempts within a specified time.

FreeBSD ports: security/sshit

http://anp.ath.cx/sshit/

symon

symon is a system monitor for obtaining accurate and up-to-date in-formation (including PF packet filter and ALTQ queue statistics) on the performance and usage of a number of systems. A symon "probe" can send measured data to a symux and the symux will store the data in RRD files which can be used to generate graphs via rrdtool or a symon-specific web-frontend called syweb.

FreeBSD ports: sysutils/symon

http://www.xs4all.nl/~wpd/symon/

TinyBSD

TinyBSD is a set of shell scripts designed to allow easy development of embedded systems based on FreeBSD. It includes configurations for generating a firewall system image providing PF.

FreeBSD ports: sysutils/tinybsd

http://www.tinybsd.org/

Index

Colophon

This book was generated using L$_Y$X 1.4.2 (using QT3 interface), TeT$_E$X 3.0, and the Koma-script book class (scrbook). The original HTML files were converted using html2latex 1.1, but mostly manually modified.

The graphics were layed out using Inkscape 0.43. Public domain clipart was used from the Open Clip Art Library (http://openclipart.org/).

The software was provided using the pkgsrc packaging system. The operating system used to do this layout and editing was NetBSD/i386. (while PF research was performed on various BSD platforms).

CPSIA information can be obtained
at www.ICGtesting.com
Printed in the USA
FSOW01n2057281116
27933FS